MERGERS AND ACQUISITIONS

CASES AND MATERIALS

WILLIAM J. CARNEY
Charles Howard Candler Professor
Emory University School of Law

2010 SUPPLEMENT

New York, New York
Foundation Press
2010

© 2008, 2009 THOMSON REUTERS/FOUNDATION PRESS
© 2010 By THOMSON REUTERS/FOUNDATION PRESS
        1 New York Plaza, 34th Floor
        New York, NY 10004
        Phone Toll Free 1–877–888–1330
        Fax 646–424–5201
        foundation–press.com
Printed in the United States of America

ISBN 978–1–59941–796–7

Mat #40973349

TABLE OF CONTENTS

The page number at which the new material appears in this Supplement is indicated in the right column; the page number of the Casebook at which I suggest the new material should be considered appears in the left column.

Chapter Eleven

Insert at page 64, immediately before "Accounting for Partial Acquisitions":

In December 2007 FASB issued SFAS No. 141 (revised 2007) to clarify some issues remaining from the 2001 revision. It takes effect for transactions on or after the beginning of the first fiscal year beginning on or after December 15, 2008, which means that for most companies the effective date is January 1, 2009. Even in mergers of equals, it requires recognition of one entity as the acquiring firm. It provides greater specificity about measurement of value of assets acquired, requires valuation of certain contingent liabilities and assets, requires measurement of contingent payments and inclusion of those amounts in calculating the purchase price. It also provides that as new information becomes available during the fiscal year about values as of the closing date, adjustments are to be made (excluding new developments or events). In the case of a bargain purchase, where the seller is under some duress, it recognizes the concept of "negative goodwill" to the extent the net value of the assets acquired exceeds the purchase price. Such "negative goodwill is recognized by the buyer in income in the year of the acquisition.

Insert at page 87, immediately before "Note."

Crown EMAK Partners, LLC v. Kurz
2010 Del. LEXIS 182 (Del. Supr. 2010)

HOLLAND, Justice:

This is a consolidated appeal from a final judgment entered by the Court of Chancery pursuant to Rule 54(b). This proceeding involves competing requests for relief under section 225 of the Delaware General Corporation Law (the "DGCL"). At issue is which of two competing factions lawfully controls the board of directors (the "Board") of EMAK Worldwide, Inc. ("EMAK").

Prior to December 18, 2009, the Board had six directors and one vacancy. On December 18, one director resigned, creating a second vacancy. The plaintiffs-appellees contend that on December 20 and 21, Take Back EMAK, LLC ("TBE") delivered sufficient consents (the "TBE Consents") to remove two additional directors without cause, and fill three of the resulting vacancies with Philip Kleweno, Michael Konig, and Lloyd Sems. Incumbent director Donald A. Kurz ("Kurz") is a member of TBE. If valid, the TBE Consents would establish a new Board majority.

The defendants-appellants contend that on December 18, 2009, Crown EMAK Partners, LLC ("Crown") delivered sufficient consents (the "Crown Consents") to amend EMAK's bylaws (the "Bylaw Amendments") in two important ways. First, the Crown Consents purportedly amended Section 3.1 of the Bylaws

("New Section 3.1") to reduce the size of the Board to three directors. Because Crown has the right to appoint two directors under the terms of EMAK's Series AA Preferred Stock, a by-law reducing the Board to three, if valid, would give Crown a Board majority. Second, the Crown Consents purportedly added a new Section 3.1.1 to the Bylaws ("New Section 3.1.1") providing that if the number of sitting directors exceeds three, then the EMAK CEO will call a special meeting of stockholders to elect the third director, who will take office as the singular successor to his multiple predecessors. The defendants contend that the Bylaw amendments are valid and that the next step is for the EMAK CEO to call a special meeting under New Section 3.1.1.

The Court of Chancery concluded that the TBE Consents validly effected corporate action and that, therefore, the lawful Board consists of incumbent directors Kurz, Jeffrey Deutschman, and Jason Ackerman, and newly elected directors Kleweno, Konig, and Sems. Consequently, one vacancy remains. The Court of Chancery also concluded that the bylaw amendments adopted through the Crown Consents conflict with the DGCL and are void. Therefore, the court held, the Crown Consents were ineffective either to reduce the size of the Board or to require the calling of a special meeting.

The appellants raise three claims in this appeal. First, the appellants submit that the Court of Chancery erred in concluding that Kurz did not engage in impermissible vote buying. In the alternative, they contend Kurz's purported purchase of the outcome determinative shares from Peter Boutros ("Boutros") was an improper transfer under the plain language of a Restricted Stock Grant Agreement between EMAK and Boutros. Second, they argue that the Court of Chancery erred when it held that Cede breakdowns should be deemed part of the "stock ledger" under title 8, section 219 of the Delaware Code with the result that the member depository banks and brokers are record holders. They submit that a proxy from DTC, as the only undisputed record holder of shares in "street name," was required to count the votes of those banks and brokers. Since TBE failed to obtain a proxy from DTC, those votes were invalid and improperly counted. Third, they argue that the Court of Chancery erred when it held that the Crown Consent was void because the amendments to the bylaws conflict with Delaware law.

We hold that Kurz did not engage in improper vote buying, but that his purchase of shares from Boutros was an improper transfer that was prohibited by a restricted stock agreement between Boutros and EMAK. Because the Boutros shares could not be voted, that deprived the Kurz faction of the votes required to elect their nominees. We therefore do not reach the issue of whether the Cede breakdowns are part of the "stock ledger" under title 8, section 291 of the Delaware Code. For reasons more fully discussed in this opinion, the Court of Chancery's interpretation of "stock ledger" under section 219 should be regarded as *obiter dictum* and without precedential effect. Finally, we hold that the Crown bylaw amendments were invalid because they conflict with Delaware law.

Therefore, the judgments of the Court of Chancery are affirmed in part and reversed in part. This matter is remanded for further proceedings in accordance with this opinion.

Factual Background

EMAK's Capital Structure

EMAK is a Delaware corporation based in Los Angeles, California. EMAK has two classes of stock: common shares and the Series AA Preferred Stock.

EMAK has issued and outstanding 7,034,322 shares of common stock. EMAK's common shares traded on NASDAQ from 1994 until April 14, 2008, when trading was suspended. On June 17, 2008, EMAK was delisted. EMAK subsequently deregistered, although its common shares continue to trade on the pink sheets.

EMAK has issued and outstanding 25,000 shares of Series AA Preferred Stock, all held by Crown. The Series AA Preferred has the right to elect two directors to the Board, plus a third director if the Board expands to more than eight members. The Series AA Preferred does not vote in the election of directors. It does vote on an as-converted basis with the common stock on all other matters. The Series AA Preferred can convert into 2,777,777 common shares and carries 27.6% of EMAK's total voting power on matters where it votes with the common stock.

TBE Consent Solicitation And Exchange Transaction

On Monday, October 12, 2009, TBE delivered an initial consent to EMAK, thereby launching its consent solicitation (the "TBE Consent Solicitation"). Under Section 2.13© of EMAK's bylaws (the "Bylaws"), the Board had the power to set a record date for the TBE Consent Solicitation. During a meeting held on October 19, the Board set October 22 as the record date. Had the Board not exercised its authority, the record date would have been October 12, the date of delivery of the initial TBE Consent.

*   *   *

Three Simultaneous Consent Solicitations

During December 2009, solicitation activity intensified, because three simultaneous consent solicitations were under way. TBE continued its solicitation activities and issued a series of press releases and public statements in support of the TBE Consent Solicitation. On December 7, EMAK began soliciting consent revocations and issued a series of press releases and public statements in support of its efforts.

. . . . Crown designated Jason Ackerman as the second director authorized by the Series AA Preferred Stock.

*   *   *

DTC's And Broadridge's Roles in TBE Consent Solicitation

TBE conducted a broad-based solicitation in which it sought to obtain consents from a large number of individual EMAK stockholders. Since EMAK's shares were publicly traded for fourteen years, a significant number of EMAK stockholders owned their shares in "street name." This practice is summarized in a leading treatise:

> The vast majority of publicly traded shares in the United States are registered on the companies' books not in the name of beneficial owners--*i.e.*, those investors who paid for, and have the right to vote and dispose of, the shares--but rather in the name of "Cede & Co.," the name used by The Depository Trust Company ("DTC").

> Shares registered in this manner are commonly referred to as being held in "street name." . . . DTC holds the shares on behalf of banks and brokers, which in turn hold on behalf of their clients (who are the underlying beneficial owners or other intermediaries).[3]

The roles of DTC and the Investor Communications Solutions Division of Broadridge Financial Services, Inc. ("Broadridge") are important in this case. Broadridge's role has been summarized as follows:

> For many years, banks and brokers maintained their own proxy departments to handle the back-office administrative processes of distributing proxy materials and tabulating voting instructions from their clients. Today, however, the overwhelming majority have eliminated their proxy departments and subcontracted these processes out to [Broadridge]. For many years, these proxy processing services were provided by Automatic Data Processing, Inc. ("ADP"), but on March 31, 2007, ADP spun off its Brokerage Services Group into a new independent company, Broadridge, which now provides these services to most banks and brokers.

> To make these arrangements work, Broadridge's bank and broker clients formally transfer to Broadridge the proxy authority they receive from DTC (via the [DTC] Omnibus Proxy) via written powers of attorney. On behalf of the brokers and banks, Broadridge delivers directly to each beneficial owner a proxy statement and, importantly, a voting instruction form (referred to as a "VIF") rather than a proxy card. Beneficial owners do not receive proxy cards because they are not vested with the right to vote shares or to grant proxy authority--those rights belong only to the legal owners (or their designees). Beneficial owners merely have the right to instruct how their shares are to be voted by Broadridge (attorney-in-fact of

---

[3]   John C. Wilcox, John J. Purcell III, & Hye-Won Choi, *"Street Name" Registration & The Proxy Solicitation Process* in Amy Goodman, et al., *A Practical Guide to SEC Proxy and Compensation Rules* 10-3 (4th ed. 2007 & 2008 Supp.).

the DTC participants), which they accomplish by returning a VIF.[4]

DTC is generally regarded as the entity having the power under Delaware law to vote the shares that it holds on deposit for the banks and brokers who are members of DTC. Through the DTC omnibus proxy, DTC transfers its voting authority to those member banks and brokers. The banks and brokers then transfer the voting authority to Broadridge, which votes the shares held at DTC by each bank and broker in proportion to the aggregate voting instructions received from the ultimate beneficial owners.

For the TBE Consent Solicitation, Broadridge collected, recorded, and totaled the voting instructions it received from the beneficial owners of EMAK shares held in street name. There is no dispute that the banks and brokers properly authorized Broadridge to vote the EMAK shares held on their behalf by DTC.[*]

What no one ever obtained, and what DTC never provided, was the DTC omnibus proxy. The evidence conflicts as to who had the responsibility to get the DTC omnibus proxy. The Court of Chancery found that neither party clearly had the obligation to secure the DTC omnibus proxy, although both could have done more, neither acted improperly or inequitably with respect to this aspect of the case.

Delivery of the Consents

On December 18, 2009, Crown delivered the Crown Consents to EMAK, along with a certification required by Section 2.13(e) of the Bylaws attesting to Crown's good faith belief that Crown had received sufficient consents to take corporate action. Given the nearly 28% voting power that Crown could wield on matters other than the election of directors, Crown needed only another 23% to reach the necessary majority of EMAK's outstanding voting power. Crown obtained

---

[4]   *Id.* at 10-14.

[*]   "Because DTCC's role is only that of custodian, a number of mechanisms have been developed in order to pass the legal rights it holds as the record owner (such as the right to vote) to the beneficial owners. The first step in passing voting rights down the chain is the "omnibus proxy," which DTCC executes to transfer its voting rights to its participant nominees.

"Under applicable rules, nominees must deliver proxy materials to beneficial owners and request voting instructions. Nominees are often prohibited by applicable New York Stock Exchange ("NYSE"), or other self-regulatory organization ("SRO") rules, or by express agreements with their customers from voting the securitiesheld in their customers' accounts in the absence of receiving such customers' voting instructions.

"A large number of nominees have contracted out the administrative processes of distributing proxy materials and tabulating voting instructions to us. Nominees accomplish this by transferring to us via powers of attorney the authority to execute a proxy, which authority they receive from DTCC (via omnibus proxy). We then distribute the proxy materials and voting instruction forms (known as "VIFs") to beneficial owners."
Broadridge 2009 Form 10-K, pages 3-4 at
http://www.broadridge-ir.com/fin/annual/br_AR2009.pdf (last viewed 5/1/10). - Ed.

that majority from EMAK management and one large institutional holder. With only a few consents to deliver, Crown sidestepped the need for a DTC omnibus proxy by having DTC execute the consents in the name of Cede & Co., a procedure DTC offers to beneficial holders akin to the issuance of appraisal demands in Cede's name. This approach is not practical for a broad-based solicitation such as that which TBE conducted.

Boutros Purchase Agreement

With the December 21, 2009, deadline looming, TBE and its principals were working feverishly to round up the final consents. On Thursday, December 17, Sems emailed Kurz: "We need to buy someone[s'] shares this weekend."

One person whose vote remained undecided was Boutros, a former employee and current consultant of EMAK who lived in Australia. Boutros owned 175,000 shares of restricted stock, all entitled to vote. Both sides sought Boutros's support. On Thursday, December 17, 2009, Boutros told Kurz that he would support Crown. Kurz responded that he would contact Boutros that weekend and encouraged Boutros to reconsider before the December 21 deadline.

As of Friday, December 18, 2009, D.F. King, TBE's proxy solicitor, showed TBE having consents for approximately 48.4% of the common shares. To prevail, TBE needed another 116,325 votes.

Between Friday, December 18 and Sunday, December 20, 2009, Kurz had a series of telephone calls with Boutros. On Sunday, Kurz had additional calls with Boutros's counsel. The result was a Purchase Agreement dated as of December 20, 2009 (the "Purchase Agreement"), in which Boutros sold to Kurz:

> (a) all shares of common stock of EMAK Worldwide, Inc., a Delaware corporation (the "Company") that Seller owns and is entitled or permitted to sell, transfer or assign as of the date hereof (the "Shares"), and (b) all rights to receive all other shares of the Company that the Seller is or may hereafter be entitled or permitted to sell, transfer or assign, for a total purchase price of U.S. $ 225,000.00 (the "Purchase Price"), with the Purchase Price to be paid by wire transfer to an account designated by Seller upon full execution of this Agreement.

Boutros originally asked for $ 2.25 per share. Kurz felt that was too high and bargained Boutros down. Kurz believed he obtained the economic and voting rights (albeit not legal title) to 150,000 shares, resulting in a price of $ 1.50 per share. At the time, EMAK's stock was trading on the pink sheets for around $ 0.95 per share.

*   *   *

Section 2 of the Purchase Agreement was critical to Kurz. It provides:

> **Proxies**. As a material part of the consideration for this Agreement, and an express condition precedent to the effectiveness hereof, Seller agrees to execute and deliver to Buyer by facsimile transmittal on the date

hereof, time being of the essence, with originals to follow immediately by express delivery, (a) this Agreement, (b) an Irrevocable Proxy, © the Revocation, and (d) the White Consent Card solicited by Take Back EMAK, LLC, each in the form attached hereto.

With Boutros' votes in hand, Kurz believed TBE had the consents it needed to prevail.

Late in the evening on December 20, 2009, Kurz's counsel sent by email to EMAK's general counsel an initial Broadridge omnibus consent dated November 23, 2009, reflecting voting instructions received through that date (the "Initial Broadridge Omnibus Consent"). Kurz's counsel also sent written consent cards for record holders and a certification attesting to the soliciting parties' good faith belief that they had received valid and unrevoked consents sufficient to take corporate action. The defendants-appellants question whether Kurz, TBE, and the other soliciting parties could have held that good faith belief on December 20. The Court of Chancery found that the certification was properly given, based on the consents TBE had in hand and the information TBE had from its proxy solicitor about how the street name vote came in.

On the morning of December 21, 2009, the same documents were hand-delivered to EMAK's registered office in Delaware. That morning, TBE ordered a supplemental omnibus consent from Broadridge dated December 21, 2009 (the "Supplemental Broadridge Omnibus Consent"), showing additional votes, net of revocations, since November 23. The Supplemental Broadridge Omnibus Consent was hand-delivered to EMAK's registered office later that day. TBE also delivered additional consent cards from registered holders to EMAK's registered office.

The IVS Reports

* * *

On December 23, 2009, IVS issued its preliminary tabulation report on the TBE Consents. IVS reported that record holders of 2,496,598 shares expressed consent in favor of the TBE Consent Solicitation and that street name holders of 1,055,815 shares consented through the Broadridge omnibus consents. The combined tally of 3,552,413 shares represented a majority of the 7,034,322 common shares outstanding on the record date. The IVS preliminary report, however, treated the street votes as "invalid due to the lack of a DTC omnibus proxy on file."

On January 14, 2010, TBE delivered a written challenge to the IVS preliminary report. TBE contended that (i) the consents for shares held in street name should be counted and (ii) the tally in favor of TBE should include additional consents delivered on December 21, 2009.

On January 15, 2010, IVS issued its final report. IVS revised its tally to take into account consent cards delivered on December 21, 2009, and now reported that record holders of 2,502,032 shares expressed consents in favor of the TBE Consent Solicitation. IVS declined to count the street name consents, however.

As of October 22, 2009, EMAK had 7,034,322 shares outstanding. In order to prevail, TBE needed to obtain consents for 3,517,162 shares (50% + 1). Backing out the consents for 2,502,032 shares that TBE received from record holders would leave a balance of 1,015,130 votes required for victory.

The IVS preliminary report showed that TBE received consents from street name holders of 1,055,815 shares, which was more than sufficient. Table A shows for each proposal (i) the votes received by TBE through the Initial Broadridge Omnibus Consent and (ii) the additional votes, net of revocations, received by TBE through the Supplemental Broadridge Omnibus Consent. On each issue, the Broadridge omnibus consents provided TBE with sufficient votes from shares held in street name for TBE to prevail.

TABLE A

Issue	Initial Broadridge Omnibus Consent	Supplemental Broadridge Omnibus Consent	Total
Removal of incumbent directors	1,055,815	3,144	1,058,959
Elect Kleweno	1,055,965	4,634	1,060,599
Elect Konig	1,055,965	2,287	1,058,252
Elect Sems	1,055,965	2,287	1,058,252

*   *   *

The Court of Chancery found it necessary, however, to review the number of shares voted by the Broadridge omnibus consents and count only the number of shares actually held by the banks and brokers on the true record date of October 22, 2009. If DTC holds shares of a corporation on behalf of banks and brokers, then the corporation can ask DTC to provide what is technically known as a participant listing and informally referred to as a "Cede breakdown." The Cede breakdown for a particular date identifies by name each bank or broker that holds shares with DTC as of that date and the number of shares held, respectively, by each. In contrast to the DTC omnibus proxy, which is not governed by any legal authority, federal regulations require DTC to furnish a Cede breakdown promptly when an issuer corporation requests it.

In November 2009, EMAK obtained Cede breakdowns for both October 12 and October 22. The Cede breakdowns show the aggregate decline in the share positions of each of the thirty-one banks and brokers who held EMAK shares through DTC. The total reduction was 29,386 shares, less than the margin of victory on each issue. (The same calculation can be derived by cutting back the overvote on a broker-by-broker basis.) Assuming conservatively that even if TBE lost one consent for each share by which the position of a consenting bank or broker declined, TBE still prevailed. Table B shows the calculations.

TABLE B

Issue	Total Street Votes From Broadridge Omnibus Consents	Total Votes After Reduction of 29,386 Shares	Margin of Victory Based On 1,015,130 Street Votes Needed
Removal of incumbent directors	1,058,959	1,029,573	14,443
Elect Kleweno	1,060,599	1,031,213	16,083
Elect Konig	1,058,252	1,028,866	13,736
Elect Sems	1,058,252	1,028,866	13,736

The Court of Chancery found, as fact, that if all of the TBE Consents are counted, including the street votes from the Broadridge omnibus consents, then TBE delivered sufficient consents to EMAK to take valid corporate action.

Analysis

Improper Vote Buying Concern

Shareholder voting differs from voting in public elections, in that the shares on which the shareholders' vote depends can be bought and sold. Vote buying in the context of corporate elections and other shareholder actions has been and continues to be an important issue. Several commentators have addressed the corporate voting process and techniques by which shareholder voting rights can be manipulated.

The Court of Chancery characterized vote buying that does not involve the use of corporate resources as "third party vote buying." Here, although Kurz is a director of EMAK, he used his own resources to acquire Boutros's shares. Accordingly, Kurz's actions as a third party do not involve the problem of insiders using corporate resources to "buy" votes.

Vote buying has been described as disenfranchising when it delivers the swing votes. In this case, the Court of Chancery opined that third party vote buying merits judicial review if it is disenfranchising, *i.e.*, if it actually affects the outcome of the vote. [10] Applying those principles to this case, the Court of Chancery concluded that the Purchase Agreement between Kurz and Boutros was potentially disenfranchising and "should be subjected to a vote buying analysis," because the "Purchase Agreement provided TBE with the votes they needed to prevail and disenfranchised what would have been a silent majority against the TBE Consent Solicitation." Therefore, it determined that the Purchase Agreement should be scrutinized closely.

The Court of Chancery noted a 1983 scholarly analysis of shareholder voting which concluded " it is not possible to separate the voting right from the equity interest" and that "[s]omeone who wants to buy a vote must buy the stock too." [11] The Court of Chancery also recognized, however, that over the last twenty-five years "[i]nnovations in technology and finance have made it easier to separate voting from the financial claims of shares."[12] Today, "the market permits providers to slice and dice the shareholder's interest in a variety of ways, and investors are willing to buy these separate interests."

According to a recent scholarly study of corporate voting by Professors Robert Thompson and Paul Edelman, a disconnect between voting rights and the economic interests of shares "compromises the ability of voting to perform its assigned role." They concluded that "[a] decisionmaking system that relies on votes to determine the decision of the group necessarily requires that the voters' interest be aligned with the collective interest. [Therefore, i]t remains important to require an alignment between share voting and the financial interest of the shares."

No Improper Vote Buying

For many years, Delaware decisions have expressed consistent concerns about transactions that create a misalignment between the voting interest and the economic interest of shares. As then Vice-Chancellor (now Chief Justice) Steele explained, "[g]enerally speaking, courts closely scrutinize vote-buying because a shareholder who divorces property interest from voting interest [] fails to serve the 'community of interest' among all shareholders, since the 'bought' shareholder votes may not reflect rational, economic self-interest arguably common to all shareholders." Again, in this case, the Court of Chancery recognized that "[w]hat legitimizes the stockholder vote as a decision-making mechanism is the premise that stockholders with economic ownership are expressing their collective view as to whether a particular course of action serves the corporate goal of stockholder wealth maximization."[17]

Accordingly, the Court of Chancery held that "[p]olicing third-party vote buying does not rest on the outdated notion that every stockholder owes every other stockholder a duty to use its best judgment while voting. It flows instead from the

---

[11]   Frank H. Easterbrook & Daniel R. Fischel, *Voting in Corporate Law*, 26 J. L. & Econ. 395, 410(1983).

[12]   12 Robert B. Thompson & Paul H. Edelman, *Corporate Voting*, 62 Vand. L. Rev. 129, 153 (2009).

[17]   A Delaware public policy of guarding against the decoupling of economic ownership from voting power can be seen in the 2009 amendment to section 213(a), which now authorizes a board to set one record date for purposes of giving notice of a meeting of stockholders and a second, later record date for determining which stockholders can vote at the meeting. Del. Code Ann. tit. 8, § 213(a) (West Supp. 2010).

legitimating conditions necessary for meaningful stockholder voting. . . ." The Court of Chancery concluded that:

> Because transactions in which economic interests are fully aligned with voting rights do not raise concern, Delaware law does not restrict a soliciting party from buying shares and getting a proxy to bolster the solicitation's chance of success. Delaware law presumes that in the sale of the underlying stock, the seller sells and assigns all of its rights, title and interest, "including its right to grant a consent or a revocation with respect to a past record date. . . ." *Commonwealth Assocs. v. Providence Health Care*, 641 A.2d at 158. Delaware law further presumes that "upon request the seller will, in good faith, take such ministerial steps as are necessary (*e.g.*, granting proxies) to effectuate the transfer." *Id.* Such transactions are common. John C. Wilcox, John J. Purcell III, & Hye-Won Choi, *"Street Name" Registration & The Proxy Solicitation Process*, at 10-26 in Amy Goodman, et al., *A Practical Guide to SEC Proxy and Compensation Rules* (4th Ed. 2007 & 2008 Supp.) ("[O]ver the course of a proxy contest, it is not uncommon for contestants to attempt to increase their voting power by purchasing additional shares . . . ."); Robert B. Thompson & Paul H. Edelman, *Corporate Voting*, 62 Vand. L. Rev. 129, 130 (2009) ("A corporate voter who has intense feelings about the matter to be determined can influence, if not control, the outcome by purchasing shares.").

Guided by these principles, the Court of Chancery scrutinized the Purchase Agreement as follows:

> I find no evidence of fraud in the transaction. The record indicates that Boutros was fully informed about the ongoing consent solicitations. Both factions had made multiple attempts to get him to commit to their side. Although there is no direct evidence establishing that Boutros knew his shares were the swing shares, I conclude that he must have been cognizant of this fact. He cut his deal with Kurz over the weekend before the Monday on which the TBE Consent Solicitation ended. At a time when EMAK's stock was trading on the pink sheets for less than a dollar, Boutros asked for $ 2.25 per share and received $ 1.50 per share. Boutros was advised by counsel and bargained to obtain specific terms for the deal, including an absence of representations and warranties and contractual indemnification from Kurz. These are the hallmarks of a transaction in which Boutros understood what he was selling, the circumstances under which he was selling it, and what he was getting in return.

> This brings me to the *alignment of interests*. Although Kurz did not take title to the 150,000 shares that Boutros owned, and although I assume the Restricted Stock Grant Agreement prohibits Boutros from transferring title to Kurz until March 3, 2011, Boutros nevertheless transferred to Kurz,

and *Kurz now bears, 100% of the economic risk* from the 150,000 shares. If the value of EMAK's shares drops further, then Kurz will suffer. If EMAK goes bankrupt and its shares become worthless, then Kurz will have a paper souvenir. Conversely, if EMAK turns itself around and prospers, then Kurz will benefit. Kurz has already paid Boutros. Kurz's only interest lies in how EMAK performs.

Because Kurz now holds the economic interest in the shares, Delaware law presumes that he should and will exercise the right to vote. Commonwealth Assocs. v. Providence Health Care, 641 A.2d at 158; *see Len v. Fuller*, 1997 Del. Ch. LEXIS 78, 1997 WL 305833, at *5 (Del. Ch. May 30, 1997) (barring record holder from voting shares by written consent after corporation exercised option to acquire shares); *Freeman v. Fabiniak*, 1985 Del. Ch. LEXIS 486, 1985 WL 11583, at *7 (Del. Ch. Aug. 15, 1985) ("[I]t would be inequitable to allow a holder of record who holds mere legal title to stock to act by consent in a manner contrary to the wishes of the true owner."). The proxy Boutros granted to Kurz under the Purchase Agreement comports with what our law expects. *See generally* John C. Wilcox, John J. Purcell III, & Hye-Won Choi, *"Street Name" Registration & The Proxy Solicitation Process* at 10-27 in Amy Goodman, et al., *A Practical Guide to SEC Proxy and Compensation Rules* 10-3 (4th ed. 2007 & 2008 Supp.) (explaining that a purchaser typically obtains an irrevocable proxy when shares are acquired from a registered holder).

We hold that the Court of Chancery correctly concluded that there was no improper vote buying, because the economic interests and the voting interests of the shares remained aligned since both sets of interests were transferred from Boutros to Kurz by the Purchase Agreement.

Restricted Stock Grant Agreement Violated

[The court held that Boutros had no contractual right to transfer his restricted shares, and thus the purchase agreement did not act as a legally valid sale of his shares to Kurz.]

Written Consent Must Be Executed by a Record Holder

The defendants also argue the TBE Consents cannot be effective because of the absence of a DTC omnibus proxy. Section 228(a) of the DGCL provides:

Unless otherwise provided in the certificate of incorporation, any action required by this chapter to be taken at any annual or special meeting of stockholders of a corporation, or any action which may be taken at any annual or special meeting of such stockholders, may be taken without a meeting, without prior notice and without a vote, if a consent or consents in writing, setting forth the action so taken, shall be signed *by the holders of outstanding stock having not less than the minimum number of votes that would be necessary to authorize or take such action at a meeting at which all shares entitled to vote thereon were present and voted* and shall be delivered to the corporation by delivery to its registered office in this State, its principal place of business or an officer or agent of the corporation having custody of the book in which proceedings of meetings of stockholders are recorded.

Section 228© requires that each consent "bear the date of signature of each stockholder" and that to be effective, consents "signed by a sufficient number of holders" must be delivered to the corporation "within 60 days of the earliest dated consent."

In the Court of Chancery, the plaintiffs' initial response to the lack of a DTC omnibus proxy was to argue that a written consent need not be executed by a stockholder of record. In two decisions, *Freeman v. Fabiniak*[26] and *Grynberg v. Burke*,[27] the Court of Chancery previously held that only a stockholder of record can execute a written consent. The plaintiffs asked the Court of Chancery not to follow the holdings in those prior opinions, which the plaintiffs contend "betray an unfounded hostility towards the then-novel use of written consents in control contests and an unjustified preference for the traditional stockholder meeting."[28] In this case, the Court of Chancery rejected the plaintiffs' arguments "both as a matter of statutory analysis and for policy reasons." Instead it adhered to the holdings of *Freeman* and *Grynberg* that only a stockholder of record can execute a written consent.

Section 219(c) of the DGCL provides that "[t]he stock ledger shall be the only evidence as to who are the stockholders entitled by this section . . . to vote in person or by proxy at any meeting of stockholders." "The ledger is a compilation of the transfers by and to each individual shareholder, with each transaction separately posted to separately maintained shareholder accounts." The ledger is different from a stocklist, which is "a compilation of the currently effective entries in the stock ledger." Under Section 219(a), "at least 10 days before every meeting of stockholders," the officer in charge of the stock ledger must "prepare and make . . . a complete list of the stockholders entitled to vote at the meeting."

More than fifty years ago, this Court held that only registered stockholders may exercise the power to vote in a Delaware corporation.[33] In the *American*

---

[26]   *Freeman v. Fabiniak*, 1985 Del. Ch. LEXIS 486, 1985 WL 11583 (Del. Ch. Aug. 15, 1985).

[27]   *Grynberg v. Burke*, 1981 Del. Ch. LEXIS 487, 1981 WL 17034 (Del. Ch. Aug. 13, 1981).

[33]   Am. *Hardware Corp. v. Savage Arms Corp.*, 37 Del. Ch. 59, 136 A.2d 690, 692 (Del. 1957); *accord In re Giant Portland Cement Co.*, 26 Del. Ch. 32, 21 A.2d 697, 701 (Del. Ch. 1941) ("The right to vote shares of corporate stock, having voting powers, has always been incident to its legal ownership."); *Atterbury v. Consol. Coppermines Corp.*, 26 Del. Ch. 1, 20 A.2d 743, 749 (Del. Ch. 1941) ("[T]he corporation will recognize the registered owner as the true owner . . . .").

Hardware case, Savage Arms sought stockholder approval of a stock-for-stock acquisition and sent out the notice of meeting and proxy statement sixteen days before the meeting date. American Hardware objected, arguing that "because one-third of the outstanding shares were held in brokers' accounts, the time allowed for all the stockholders to receive and consider the opposition's proxy material was insufficient." This Court rejected that argument, stating that "[t]he answer to this point is simple."

> Under the General Corporation Law, no one but a registered stockholder is, as a matter of right, entitled to vote, with certain exceptions not pertinent here. If an owner of stock chooses to register his shares in the name of a nominee, he takes the risks attendant upon such an arrangement, including the risk that he may not receive notice of corporate proceedings, or be able to obtain a proxy from his nominee. The corporation, except in special cases, is entitled to recognize the exclusive right of the registered owner to vote . . . . The corporation has ordinarily discharged its obligation under Delaware law when it mails notice to the record owner.

Section 228(a) incorporates the concept of record ownership that governs voting at a meeting of stockholders by framing the taking of action by written consent in terms of the holders of outstanding stock who would have sufficient votes to take similar action at a meeting where all shares entitled to vote are present. In this case, the Court of Chancery held "section 228 is thus appropriately interpreted as requiring that a written consent be executed by a stockholder of record." The Court of Chancery also relied on section 228(e) to reinforce that interpretation.

Section 228(e) requires that prompt notice of corporate action taken by less than unanimous written consent be provided to non-consenting stockholders "who, if the action had been taken at a meeting, would have been entitled to notice of the meeting if the record date for notice of such meeting had been the date that written consents signed by a sufficient number of holders . . . were delivered to the corporation . . . ."[38] By defining the notice obligation for written consents in terms of what would be required for a hypothetical meeting, section 228(e) strengthens the connection between voting by consent and voting at a meeting. The Court of Chancery also relied on section 212(b), which provides that "[e]ach stockholder entitled to vote at a meeting of stockholders or to express consent or dissent to corporate action in writing without a meeting may authorize another person or persons to act for such stockholder by proxy . . . ."[39]

In this case, the Court of Chancery explained why it decided to adhere to the holdings in *Freeman* and *Grynberg* that a written consent must be executed by a stockholder of record.

> By treating stockholders identically for purposes of granting proxy authority, regardless of whether the vote is at a meeting or by written consent, section 212(b) indicates that the same principles should apply in

both instances. Just as only a stockholder of record can vote at a meeting, only a stockholder of record can execute a written consent.

As a matter of Delaware public policy, there is much to be said for requiring a written consent to be executed by a record holder, which allows the corporation or an inspector of elections to determine from readily available records whether the consent was valid. Certainty and efficiency are critical values when determining how stockholder voting rights have been exercised. *Williams v. Sterling Oil of Okla., Inc.*, 273 A.2d 264, 265-66 (Del. 1971); *N. Fork Bancorp., Inc. v. Toal*, 825 A.2d 860, 868 n.19 (Del. Ch. 2000); *Blasius Indus., Inc. v. Atlas Corp.*, 564 A.2d 651, 668 (Del. Ch. 1988). This is particularly true for consents, which are effective upon delivery to the corporation of a sufficient number of valid consents.

* * *

Court of Chancery Redefines Stock Ledger

[The Court of Chancery concluded that the Cede breakdown that identifies by name each bank or broker that holds shares with DTC that is sent to issuers upon their request should be treated as part of the stock ledger for purposes of section 219(c)'s mandate that only stockholders of record can vote. The Chancery Court expressed its logic as follows: "If the Cede breakdown is part of the stock ledger, then the banks and brokers who appear on the Cede breakdown have the power to vote as record holders at a meeting of stockholders or for purposes of taking action by written consent." The Supreme Court held that while the Cede breakdown is part of the "stock list" of shareholders eligible to vote that a shareholder may demand under section 220, it is not the same as the "stock ledger" that determines eligibility to vote, and thus rejected the Chancery Court's holding, albeit as obiter dicta, because the holding that Boutros' shares were not validly transferred mooted the record shareholder issue. Without the Boutros shares Kurz and TBE lacked a majority of the votes.

[The court also rejected Crown EMAK's bylaw amendments as violating Delaware law.]

Conclusion

The judgments of the Court of Chancery are affirmed in part and reversed in part. This matter is remanded for further proceedings in accordance with this opinion. The mandate shall issue immediately.

Insert at page 88, immediately before "2. Short Form Mergers":

Note on Choice of Law for California-Based Foreign Corporations

Voting rules in mergers become confusing when one of the entities is based in California but incorporated elsewhere. California, unlike virtually all other states, does not strictly follow the Internal Affairs Doctrine of choice of law, which dictates that the law of the state of incorporation will govern relationships among the officers, directors, shareholders and the corporation. This rule is codified in MBCA §15.05©. The difficulties for transactional lawyers began with Western Air Lines, Inc. v. Sobieski, 191 Cal. App.2d 399, 12 Cal. Rptr. 719 (1961). Western, a Delaware corporation (subsequently acquired by Delta Air Lines), had 30% of its shares held by California residents and its operational center in California. Western's board proposed to eliminate cumulative voting after an insurgent group sought board seats, and prepared to solicit proxies from its shareholders to approve the amendment to its certificate of incorporation. Sobieski, the Corporations Commissioner of California, asserted that elimination of cumulative voting constituted an exchange of a new class of shares for the outstanding shares, which subjected the transaction to the California Securities Act, which gave the Commissioner authority to determine whether an exchange was "fair, just or equitable." He determined that it was not fair and denied a permit for the transaction. On appeal his position was sustained by the California Court of Appeals. Western argued that this amendment and the vote to obtain its approval were part of the internal affairs of the corporation, and thus subject only to Delaware law. The court conceded that California had no jurisdiction over the internal affairs of a Delaware corporation, but that it had jurisdiction over a sale or exchange of stock in California. The Commissioner and the court characterized Western as "pseudo-foreign corporation," because of its significant contacts with the state.

California has codified this doctrine, expanding it from its basis under the California Securities Act, to cover "pseudo-foreign corporations" under various provisions of California law, including mergers and asset sales. Cal. Corp. Code §2115, with an exclusion for corporations with shares traded on the New York or American stock exchanges or on the NASDAQ National Market. Pseudo-foreign corporations are defined as those that conduct half their business in California as measured by a formula weighing property, payroll and sales located in California, and more than 50% of its shares are held in California. The California courts have consistently upheld the validity of these provisions against challenges under the full faith and credit clause, the commerce clause and the equal protection clause, generally finding that what was mandatory under California law was a permitted option under the law of the state of incorporation.

Delaware courts recently have taken a different view of this conflict. Examen, Inc. was a privately owned Delaware corporation headquartered in California that apparently met the "pseudo-foreign corporation" standards of California law. Examen entered into a merger agreement with Reed Elsevier, Inc., which Examen's board approved on Feb. 15, 2005 that expired on April 15, 2005.

Examen had a class of preferred stock outstanding that had no separate class voting rights in its certificate of incorporation, meaning that all shares would vote as a single group under Del. GCL §251(c). VantagePoint Venture Partners 1996, owns 83% of the preferred stock, convertible into 1.6 million common shares, in addition to the 8.6 million common shares already outstanding. On March 3, 2006, Examen filed suit in the Delaware Chancery Court seeking a declaratory judgment that its merger vote is subject only to Delaware law, and that California law does not govern. In response, on March 8 VantagePoint sued in the California courts seeking discovery to establish that Examen is subject to Cal. Corp. Code §2115, and that if it is, that separate class voting is required, which would give VantagePoint a veto power over the merger. Following the lead of the California decisions, VantagePoint argued that there was no irreconcilable conflict between the two laws, and that California law, just like the rules of stock exchanges, simply gave stockholders an additional layer of protection that is not inconsistent with Delaware law. The Chancery Court noted that VantagePoint's argument was weakened by the language of §2115(b), which provided that the listed provisions of California law "shall apply to a foreign corporation as defined in subdivision (a) (*to the exclusion of the law of the jurisdiction in which it is incorporated*)...." (Emphasis supplied.) VantagePoint responded that Delaware law permits separate class voting; it simply doesn't mandate it. The Chancery Court rejected this argument, noting that application of California law would be "in derogation of the rights of Examen's other stockholders," so that the court could not enforce both Delaware and California law. The Chancery Court treated this as a question of choice of law, and applied the internal affairs doctrine of choice of law of Delaware to hold that the law of Delaware, and not that of California, applies to a Delaware corporation.

On expedited appeal, the Delaware Supreme Court affirmed. Citing *dicta* in a case involving the validity of takeover defenses under the Commerce Clause, CTS Corp. v. Dynamics Corp. of America, 481 U.S. 69 (1987) [see page 480, *infra*], in which Justice Powell noted that the court had struck down statutes that imposed inconsistent regulations on activities. But it was not content to affirm simply on the choice of law grounds. The court noted that California's attempt to supplant the law of the state of incorporation for a pseudo-foreign corporation might apply in one year when the criteria were met, but not apply in a subsequent year, leaving a corporation uncertain about the governing law. The court held that under the Due Process Clause "directors and officers of corporations 'have a significant right to know what law will apply to their actions' and 'stockholders . . . have a right to know by what standards of accountability they may hold those managing the corporation's business and affairs,'" and that the internal affairs doctrine is mandated by constitutional principles. The opinion went on, gratuitously, to suggest that the California courts would likely agree with this analysis in light of cases such as CTS.

QUESTIONS

1.   Recall the discussion of Brady v. Bean, 221 Ill. App. 279 (1921) in
      Schreiber v. Carney, supra, where a shareholder who was also a creditor
      bought votes from another shareholder so he could vote them in favor of
      liquidation, to protect his interest as a creditor. Would that issue influence
      the Delaware courts after this decision?

2.   William D. Andrews described proxy fights for control as battles for the
      control of the perquisites of corporate office. William D. Andrews, *The
      Stockholders' Right to Equal Opportunity in the Sale of Shares,* 78 HARV. L. REV.
      505 (1965). Bayless Manning took more or less the same position. Bayless
      Manning, *Book Review,* 67 YALE L.J. 1477, 1488 (1958) (reviewing J.
      Livingston, THE AMERICAN STOCKHOLDER (1958)), describing proxy contests as
      "[l]argely irrelevant to issues of corporate policy, fought out between rival cliques
      competing for personal control of the corporate treasury and the elixir of corporate
      office...." Would this type of argument be likely to persuade a Delaware court
      that a purchase of votes was not aligned with shareholder interests?

3.   The Delaware Supreme Court held that the Chancery Court correctly
      concluded that there was no improper vote buying because the economic
      interests and the voting interests remained aligned when Kurz contracted
      to buy Boutros' shares. Would the result change if Kurz had bought a put
      contract (an option to sell the shares at a fixed price) immediately after
      buying the share from Boutros? Suppose Kurz had sold an equivalent
      amount of shares short (borrowing from another stockholder through a
      broker) before buying Boutros' shares?

Insert at page 216, after QUESTIONS:

NOTE ON EARN-OUT PROVISIONS

The O'Tool case highlights some of the perils of earn-out clauses. A
sophisticated seller will want to specify a number of protections. A recent law firm
memo discusses some of the problems that can arise:

Solving valuation issues with earnouts – clever or stupid?

By Teresa R. Tarpley, Morris Manning & Martin LLP

LEXOLOGY, by Association of Corporate Counsel, at
http://www.lexology.com/library/detail.aspx?g=7408df4c-702d-4f50-8277-4b5a
28fd3400 (last visited June 1, 2009)

Who keeps control of the business during the earnout period

The main arguments that arise in an earnout situation are over control. If a seller has a large payment coming to them that is contingent upon the target achieving a certain milestone, then eventually it will occur to the seller that the buyer may take actions to minimize the earnout payment. The buyer will argue that both parties have the same goal going forward – to make the business successful – so the seller should not concern itself about this issue, but a sophisticated seller immediately sees through this argument. Earnouts are never set up to measure the "success" of the company as a whole. They are set up with respect to very particular metrics. If a buyer can manipulate the operations to minimize the earnout payment without affecting the overall health of the enterprise, it would be in the buyer's best interest to do so. Moreover, once a transaction is closed, the target likely will be part of a larger organization that may have a different future in mind for the target and a different measure of "success" than that envisioned by the seller.

Accordingly, a sophisticated seller will start asking for certain rights and covenants, which will essentially amount to giving the seller some control over post-closing operations. This control can be asserted outright (by the seller insisting that they stay in actual control of the operations following the closing pursuant to a specified budget) or indirectly (by the seller asking the buyer to agree to a host of affirmative and negative covenants). With respect to an EBITDA earnout hurdle, for example, a seller may be focused initially on broad issues that may affect the probability of the receipt of the earnout payment, such as the state of the economy and the risk that customers may be lost due to the deal, but their focus will need to shift quickly to detailed questions, such as:

- Will the company be required to maintain any sort of advertising budget?

- Will the company be required to continue to employ any particular number of sales people?

- Will the company have to avoid extraordinary expenses?

- Will the company have to engage in certain specified collection efforts with respect to accounts?

- Will the allocation of intercompany expenses to the target be disallowed?

- Will price changes or discounts, certain marketing promotions or certain types of contracts be disallowed?

*   *   *

A seller has to think through and deal with almost every aspect of the historical business and the business during the earnout period in order to properly set up an earnout.

From the buyer's viewpoint, the buyer's objective is to own the target, and the buyer will quickly point out that it is bearing most of the risk if the target's business fails (because the earnout is generally a minority of the purchase price). Therefore, a buyer is very reluctant to give a seller continuing control over the business or to place significant restrictions on the business going forward. In addition, the buyer doesn't want to be held liable for making reasonable business decisions, even if they have the effect of reducing the earnout. Finding an acceptable balance between the seller's desire to be protected and the buyer's desire to be able to run the business as it sees fit is extremely difficult.

So, whereas in a typical sale transaction the seller wants to sell the company and walk away and the buyer wants to acquire the company and assume control, an earnout frustrates both of these goals. As an advisor in the transaction, you need to block out a significant amount of time to walk through these issues with your client. You should also show them how the earnout discussions are likely to progress and the hard choices they are going to have to make in the end. Often, the seller ends up with far less protection than they would like, and late in the negotiations they are faced with a decision as to whether to take a leap of faith or walk from the deal. Sometimes, after parties have considered these issues carefully, they decide to forego an earnout in favor of a simpler, more certain structure.

Insert at page 238, after QUESTIONS:

The low interest rates that prevailed in the first part of the twenty-first century led to a revival of the leveraged buyouts first seen in the 1980s. The buyers were private investors, generally "private equity" firms that assembled capital from institutional investors in limited partnerships. Because interest rates were at historic lows during the early years of the first decade, these investors employed large amounts of borrowings to finance their acquisitions, and to increase the returns to equity (in exchange for increased risk). Recognizing the difficulty in enforcing MAC clauses in many instances, private equity investors, in order to avoid results such as those in the IBP case, provided that if they terminated the purchase agreement without cause they would pay termination fees that were often the mirror image of the seller's termination fee commitments. These agreements had the virtue of providing that the agreed payments were the exclusive remedy of the sellers, thus capping the damages to which the buyer was exposed. A 2007 survey by the law firm Paul Hastings Janofsky & Walker revealed that two-thirds of all deals surveyed between January 2006 and May 2007 contained such reverse termination fees.

For some sellers, this apparently was not enough. United Rentals, Inc. v. Ram Holdings Corp., 937 A2.d 810 (Del. Ch. 2007) was an example. United Rentals entered into an agreement in which Ram, an entity created by Cerberus Capital Management, L.P., one of the largest private equity buyout firms. The agreement, as finally executed, contained conflicting provisions on remedies, that illustrate the kinds of provisions that were being inserted:

Section 9.10, entitled "Specific Performance," provided: [34]

The parties agree that irreparable damage would occur in the event that any of the provisions of this Agreement were not performed in accordance with their specific terms or were otherwise breached. Accordingly, (a) [RAM Holdings] and [RAM Acquisition] shall be entitled to seek an injunction or injunctions to prevent breaches of this Agreement by the Company and to enforce specifically the terms and provisions of this Agreement, in addition to any other remedy to which such party is entitled at law or in equity and (b) the Company shall be entitled to seek an injunction or injunctions to prevent breaches of this Agreement by [RAM Holdings] or [RAM Acquisition] or to enforce specifically the terms and provisions of this Agreement and the Guarantee to prevent breaches of or enforce compliance with those covenants of [RAM Holdings] or [RAM Acquisition] that require [RAM Holdings] or [RAM Acquisition] to (I) use its reasonable best efforts to obtain the Financing and satisfy the conditions to closing set forth in Section 7.1 and Section 7.3, including the covenants set forth in Section 6.8 and Section 6.10 and (ii) consummate the transactions contemplated by this Agreement, if in the case of this clause (ii), the Financing (or Alternative Financing obtained in accordance with Section 6.10(b)) is available to be drawn down by [RAM Holdings] pursuant to the terms of the applicable agreements but is not so drawn down solely as a result of [RAM Holdings] or [RAM Acquisition] refusing to do so in breach of this Agreement. The provisions of this Section 9.10 shall be subject in all respects to Section 8.2(e) hereof, which Section shall govern the rights and obligations of the parties hereto (and of [Cerberus Partners], the Parent Related Parties, and the Company Related Parties) under the circumstances provided therein.

Section 8.2(e), referred to in the specific performance provision in section 9.10, is part of Article VIII, entitled "Termination, Amendment and Waiver." Article VIII provides specific limited circumstances in which either RAM or URI can terminate the Merger Agreement and receive a $ 100 million termination fee. The relevant portion of section 8.2(e) of the Merger Agreement provides:

Notwithstanding anything to the contrary in this Agreement, including with respect to Sections 7.4 and 9.10, (I) the Company's right to terminate this

---

[34]   The Merger Agreement permits RAM to walk away from the deal in the event of a material adverse change in URI's business, but prohibits RAM from doing so based on the condition of the credit markets in this country. Section 3.1 of the Merger Agreement expressly provides that "Material Adverse Effect shall not include facts, circumstances, events, changes, effects or occurrences (i) generally affecting the economy or the financial, debt, credit or securities markets in the United States . . . ." [Footnote the court's in the preceding sentence.]

Agreement in compliance with the provisions of Sections 8.1(d)(I) and (ii) and its right to receive the Parent Termination Fee pursuant to Section 8.2© or the guarantee thereof pursuant to the Guarantee, and (ii) [RAM Holdings] right to terminate this Agreement pursuant to Section 8.1(e)(I) and (ii) and its right to receive the Company Termination Fee pursuant to Section 8.2(b) shall, in each case, be the sole and exclusive remedy, including on account of punitive damages, of (in the case of clause (I)) the Company and its subsidiaries against [RAM Holdings], [RAM Acquisition], [Cerberus Partners] or any of their respective affiliates, stockholders, general partners, limited partners, members, managers, directors, officers, employees or agents (collectively "Parent Related Parties") and (in the case of clause (ii)) [RAM Holdings] and [RAM Acquisition] against the Company or its subsidiaries, affiliates, stockholders, directors, officers, employees or agents (collectively "Company Related Parties"), for any and all loss or damage suffered as a result thereof, and upon any termination specified in clause (I) or (ii) of this Section 8.2(e) and payment of the Parent Termination Fee or Company Termination Fee, as the case may be, none of [RAM Holdings] , [RAM Acquisition], [Cerberus Partners] or any of their respective Parent Related Parties or the Company or any of the Company Related Parties shall have any further liability or obligation of any kind or nature relating to or arising out of this Agreement or the transactions contemplated by this Agreement as a result of such termination.

These conflicts were apparently the result of a "battle of forms" in which each party would strike out the other's provisions and insert its own. When Cerberus (Ram) terminated it tendered a check for the $100 million termination fee, and URI sued for specific performance. Chancellor Chandler found that both sides' interpretations of the agreement were reasonable, leaving the agreement ambiguous, and resorted to parole evidence. Where the parole evidence does not lead to an obvious interpretation, the court applied the "forthright negotiator principle":

As I recently explained to counsel in this case, the private, subjective feelings of the negotiators are irrelevant and unhelpful to the Court's consideration of a contract's meaning, because the meaning of a properly formed contract must be shared or common. That is not to say, however, that a party's subjective understanding is never instructive. On the contrary, in cases where an examination of the extrinsic evidence does not lead to an obvious, objectively reasonable conclusion, the Court may apply the forthright negotiator principle. Under this principle, the Court considers the evidence of what one party *subjectively* "believed the obligation to be, coupled with evidence that the other party knew or should have known of such belief." In other words, the forthright negotiator principle provides that, in cases where the extrinsic evidence does not lead to a single, commonly held understanding of a contract's meaning, a court may consider the subjective understanding of one party that has been objectively manifested and is known or should be known by the other party. It is with these fundamental legal principles in mind that I consider the factual record developed at trial.

937 A.2d at 835-36. In this case the Chancellor ruled that the reverse termination fee was enforceable and the specific performance provision was not.

Insert at page 277, after note on *The ConEd Decision – One Year Later*:

Note: Employee Claims as Third Party Beneficiaries

Acquisition agreements frequently provide assurances that target company employees and retirees will not suffer precipitously as a result of a change of control. Agreements may provide for continuation of employee benefits for the first year after the acquisition and that, thereafter, benefits will be no less favorable that those of employees of the acquiring firm. Employees' seniority may be protected by provisions that target employees will receive credit for their previous service in any plans that require vesting only after specified periods of employment. Some agreements will provide for continuation of severance plans for a specified period following the closing. Some agreements will also provide that annual bonuses for the year of the transition will be calculated and awarded on the basis of the target company's existing bonus plan.

Questions about who can enforce these agreement raise questions similar to those raised about shareholder standing in the Consolidated Edison decision. In Comrie v. Enterasys Networks, Inc., 2004 Del. Ch. LEXIS 196 (Del. Ch. 2004), the acquiring corporation had, pursuant to the merger agreement, provided stock options on its own stock to employees of BIT Management, Inc., the acquired corporation. The acquiring corporation was contemplating either an initial public offering ("IPO") of its stock in the near future. The acquisition agreement provided that:

> "In the event that [the parent company] determines not to pursue its current intention to cause [the acquiring firm] to undergo an initial public offering prior to December 31, 2001 or determines not to pursue its current intention to distribute the stock of [the acquiring firm] to the shareholders of [parent] (each a *"Trigger Event"*), within sixty (60) days of the Trigger Event, [the parent] shall either (I) provide equivalent substitute or replacement awards on the same terms and conditions to the former employees of [BIT]; or (ii) pay $4,620,000 in the aggregate for all Options held by the Partners and former employees of [BIT].

A Trigger Event occurred a few months after the closing of the acquisition, and the parent corporation issued replacement options, based on the value of the original options on the date of replacement, rather than on their higher value on the date of the grant of the original options. The partners who were owners of BIT and parties to the acquisition agreement brought suit for breach of contract and prevailed. But over 41% of the options were held by former BIT employees who were not parties to the agreement, which apparently did not contain a prohibition on third-party suits. Thus the employees based their claim on the theory that they were third-party beneficiaries of the contract, and entitled to enforce their rights under it. The court cited former Vice Chancellor (now Justice) Jacobs, in Madison Realty Partners 7, LLC v. AG ISA, LLC, 2001 WL 406268, at *5, for a definition of a third party beneficiary:

> To qualify as a third party beneficiary of a contract, (I) the contracting parties must have intended that the third party beneficiary benefit from the contract, (ii) the benefit must have been intended as a gift or in satisfaction of a pre-existing obligation to that person, and (iii) the intent to benefit the third party must be a material part of the parties' purpose in entering into the contract.

In this case Vice Chancellor Lamb found that the intent to benefit the employees was plain from the face of the acquisition agreement, and that the donative intent was also clear, and was a material part of the agreement. Judgment in favor of some of the employees was entered, while the court held that others were barred by releases they had signed.

Other cases deal with interpretative questions raised clauses providing that the acquisition agreement is not intended to confer any rights upon third parties. In Prouty v. Gores Technology Group, 18 Cal. Rptr.3d 178 (Cal. App. 2004), Hewlett Packard sold a subsidiary to Gores ("GTG") with a provision in section 10.5 of the stock sale agreement that the agreement "is not intended to confer upon any Person other than the Parties hereto, the Company [the H-P subsidiary, VeriFone] [and other entities not relevant here] any rights or remedies hereunder." The agreement also provided that GTG would offer employment to all VeriFone employees upon terms and benefits similar to those paid by VeriFone, except that GTG had no duty to continue any severance pay obligation that Hewlett-Packard had previously promised.

Three months later the parties amended the acquisition agreement to provide that GTG would not terminate any Verifone employees in the first 60 days after the closing, and for any employees terminated in the next 90 days would pay the same severance that they would have received from Hewlett Packard. The amendment did not address the "no third-party beneficiary" language of section 10.5. When GTG terminated VeriFone employees in violation of the amendment and the employees sued, the court was faced with the question of whether the "no third-party beneficiary" clause of section 10.5 governed an amendment to the agreement that was clearly intended to benefit VeriFone employees. The court held that the amendment was intended to grant former employees benefits they could enforce, despite the amendment's express incorporation of the "no third-party beneficiary" clause of the original agreement, on the following basis:

> "Sections 10.5 and 8(b) [of the original agreement] state generally no rights or remedies exist under the contract to third persons; section 6 [of the amendment] expressly grants rights to specific third persons regarding their employment with GTG. In this circumstance, under well established principles of contract interpretation, when a general and a particular provision are inconsistent, the particular and specific provision is paramount to the general provision. [citations omitted] Section 6 of the amendment thus is an exception to section 10.5 of the original contract and section 8(b) of the amendment [incorporating section 10.5], and plaintiffs can enforce it."

Because many retirement and benefit plans are governed by the Employee Retirement Income Security Act of 1974 ("ERISA"), employees may seek to protect their benefits by filing claims under ERISA rather than as third party beneficiaries of an acquisition agreement by which the buyer assumes responsibility for target employee benefits, including for retired employees. When Haliburton Co. acquired Dresser Industries, the acquisition agreement provided that Haliburton would cause its acquisition subsidiary that survived the merger to maintain the Dresser retiree medical plan, except to the extent that changes to the Dresser Plan were consistent with changes in the Haliburton plan. Similarly, the agreement required Haliburton to provide Dresser employees with benefits comparable to those of Haliburton employees for at least three years from the closing. The agreement contained a "no third-party beneficiary" clause, with a specific exception for Dresser-designated directors on the Haliburton board to enforce the provisions on behalf of Dresser's employees (without mention of its retirees). Four years after the closing, Haliburton decided to merge the Dresser retiree's medical plan with its own, and a year later amended the plan to eliminate virtually all medical benefits for Dresser retirees who had reached age 65 and were eligible for Medicare. The former administrator of the Dresser plan wrote the Haliburton board objecting that this violated the merger agreement, because no similar reductions were made for Haliburton retirees.

The Dresser retirees sued to enforce the terms of the merger agreement that no changes would be made to their benefits that were not also made to the Haliburton retirees' benefits. Haliburton raised the "no third-party beneficiary" language of the merger agreement as a bar to the retirees' suit, but the court held that while it might bar their suit under the contract, it did not bar their suit under ERISA, which gave them the right to enforce the terms of the plan. The court held that the plan was effectively amended by the merger to provide the "equal treatment" protection to the Dresser retirees, who prevailed on this claim. Haliburton Company Benefits Committee v. Graves, 463 F.3d 360 (5th Cir. 2006). For a more detailed discussion of these issues, see Michael S. Katzke and David E. Kahan, Recent Court Decisions Permit Employees to Enforce Merger Agreement Compensation and Benefits Covenants 10, No. 10 THE M&A LAWYER 9 (Nov. -

Dec. 2006).

Hexion Speciality Chemicals, Inc. v. Huntsman Corp.

965 A.2d 715 (Del. Ch. 2008)

Lamb, Vice Chancellor

[This dispute arose from a contested takeover battle for Huntsman, a speciality chemical company headquartered in Utah by Hexion, a subsidiary of Apollo, a private equity firm.]

Because the buyer and its parent were eager to be the winning bidder in a competitive bidding situation, they agreed to pay a substantially higher price than the competition and to commit to stringent deal terms, including no "financing out." In other words, if the financing the buyer arranged (or equivalent alternative financing) is not available at the closing, the buyer is not excused from performing under the contract. In that event, and in the absence of a material adverse effect relating to Huntsman's business as a whole, the issue becomes whether the buyer's liability to the seller for failing to close the transaction is limited to $ 325 million by contract or, instead, is, uncapped.

The answer to that question turns on whether the buyer committed a knowing and intentional breach of any of its covenants found in the merger agreement that caused damages in excess of the contractual limit. Among other things, the buyer covenanted that it would use its reasonable best efforts to take all actions and do all things "necessary, proper or advisable" to consummate the financing on the terms it had negotiated with its banks and further covenanted that it would not take any action "that could be reasonably be expected to materially impair, delay or prevent consummation" of such financing.

While the parties were engaged in obtaining the necessary regulatory approvals, the seller reported several disappointing quarterly results, missing the numbers it projected at the time the deal was signed. After receiving the seller's first quarter 2008 results, the buyer and its parent, through their counsel, began exploring options for extricating the seller from the transaction. At first, this process focused on whether the seller had suffered a material adverse effect. By early May, however, attention shifted to an exploration of the prospective solvency of the combined entity, leading them to retain the services of a well-known valuation firm to explore the possibility of obtaining an opinion that the combined entity would be insolvent. After making a number of changes to the inputs into the deal model that materially and adversely effected the viability of the transaction, and without consulting with the seller about those changes or about other business initiatives that might improve the prospective financial condition of the resulting entity, the buyer succeeded in obtaining an "insolvency" opinion. [The commitment letter with two lending banks required production of a "customary and reasonably satisfactory" solvency certificate from the Chief Financial Officer of Hexion, the Chief Financial Officer of Huntsman, or a reputable valuation firm as a condition to the banks obligation to fund the loan.]

The insolvency opinion was presented to the buyer's board of directors on June 18, 2008, and later published in a press release claiming that the merger could not be consummated because the financing would not be available due to the prospective insolvency of the combined entity and because the seller had suffered a material adverse effect, as defined in the merger agreement. The buyer and a host of its affiliated entities immediately filed the complaint in this action, alleging a belief that the merger cannot be consummated since the financing will not be available.

The complaint alleges financing will be unavailable because, (1) the amounts available under that financing are no longer sufficient to close the transaction and (2) the combined entity would be insolvent. The complaint seeks a declaration that the buyer is not obligated to consummate the merger if the combined company would be insolvent and a further declaration that its liability (and that of its affiliates) to the seller for nonconsummation of the transaction cannot exceed the $ 325 million termination fee. The complaint also seeks a declaration that the seller suffered a material adverse effect, thus excusing the buyer's obligation to close. The seller answered and filed counterclaims seeking, among other things, an order directing the buyer to specifically perform its obligations under the merger agreement.

The court conducted six days of trial on certain of the claims for declaratory and injunctive relief raised by the pleadings. In this post-trial opinion, the court finds that the seller has not suffered a material adverse effect, as defined in the merger agreement, and further concludes that the buyer has knowingly and intentionally breached numerous of its covenants under that contract. Thus, the court will grant the seller's request for an order specifically enforcing the buyer's contractual obligations to the extent permitted by the merger agreement itself.

The court also determines that it should not now rule on whether the combined entity, however it may ultimately be capitalized, would be solvent or insolvent at closing. In this connection, the court rejects the buyer's argument that it can be excused from performing its freely undertaken contractual obligations simply because its board of directors concluded that the performance of those contractual obligations risked insolvency. Instead, it was the duty of the buyer's board of directors to explore the many available options for mitigating the risk of insolvency while causing the buyer to perform its contractual obligations in good faith. If, at closing, and despite the buyer's best efforts, financing had not been available, the buyer could then have stood on its contract rights and faced no more than the contractually stipulated damages. The buyer and its parent, however, chose a different course.

*   *   *

Due to the existence of a signed agreement with Basell [the competing bidder] and Apollo's [Hexion's parent] admittedly intense desire for the deal, Huntsman had significant negotiating leverage. As a result, the merger agreement is more than usually favorable to Huntsman. For example, it contains no financing contingency and requires Hexion to use its "reasonable best efforts" to consummate the financing. In addition, the agreement expressly provides for uncapped damages in the case of a "knowing and intentional breach of any covenant" by Hexion and for liquidated damages of $ 325 million in cases of other enumerated breaches. The narrowly tailored MAE clause is one of the few ways the merger agreement allows Hexion to walk away from the deal without paying Huntsman at least $ 325 million in liquidated damages.

*   *   *

III.

Both parties seek declaratory judgment on the subject of knowing and intentional breach. Hexion seeks a declaratory judgment that no "knowing and intentional breach" of the merger agreement has occurred, and therefore its liability for any breach of the merger agreement is capped at $ 325 million. Huntsman seeks the obverse -- a declaratory judgment that Hexion has engaged in a "knowing and intentional breach" of the merger agreement, and therefore it is entitled to full contract damages, not capped or liquidated by the $ 325 million figure in section 7.3(d) of the merger agreement. For the reasons detailed below, the court concludes that Hexion has engaged in a knowing and intentional breach, and that the liquidated damages clause of section 7.3(d) is therefore inapplicable.

The court first turns to the meaning of "knowing and intentional breach" as it is used in the merger agreement. "Knowing and intentional," a phrase which echoes with notes of criminal and tort law, is not normally associated with contract law. In fact, the term does not appear at all in either WILLISTON ON CONTRACTS or the RESTATEMENT OF THE LAW OF CONTRACTS. Hexion argues in its pretrial brief that a "knowing" breach "requires that Hexion not merely know of its actions, but have *actual knowledge* that such actions *breach* the covenant," and that negligence or a mistake of law or fact will not suffice to establish a knowing breach. Moreover, it argues, for such breach to also be "intentional," Hexion must have "acted `purposely' with the `conscious object' of breaching."

Hexion commits the same fundamental error in its analysis of both terms. Hexion interprets the terms "knowing" and "intentional" as modifying the violation of the legal duty supposed, rather than modifying the act which gives rise to the violation. This is simply wrong. Momentarily drawing the analogy to criminal law which Hexion invites makes this immediately clear: it is the rare crime indeed in which knowledge of the criminality of the act is itself an element of the crime. If one man intentionally kills another, it is no defense to a charge of murder to claim that the killer was unaware that killing is unlawful. Similarly, if a man takes another's umbrella from the coat check room, it may be a defense to say he mistakenly believed the umbrella to be his own (a mistake of fact). It is no defense to say he had not realized that stealing was illegal, nor is it a defense that it was not his "purpose" to break the law, but simply to avoid getting wet. Contrary to Hexion's contention, mistake of law virtually never excuses a violation of law. [87] Hexion cites a number of cases in support of its interpretation. However, once this distinction between mistakes of fact and law is plain, it becomes equally plain that the cases Hexion cites in support of its argument are inapposite. Indeed the alternative would make "knowing and intentional breach" synonymous with willful and malicious breach, a concept ultimately having no place in an action sounding in contract rather than tort. It is a fundamental proposition of contract law that damages in contract are solely to give the non-breaching party the "benefit of the bargain," and not to punish the breaching party. [89] It is for this very reason that penalty clauses are unenforceable. [90] Instead, the best definition of "knowing and intentional breach" is the one suggested by Hexion's citation to the entry for "knowing" in Black's Law Dictionary [91] Black's lists "deliberate" as one of its definitions for knowing. [92] Thus a "knowing and intentional" breach is a deliberate one -- a breach that is a direct consequence of a deliberate act undertaken by the breaching party, rather than one which results indirectly, or as a result of the breaching party's negligence or unforeseeable misadventure. In other words, a "knowing and intentional" breach, as used in the merger agreement, is the taking of a deliberate act, which act constitutes in and of itself a breach of the merger agreement, even if breaching was not the conscious object of the act. It is with this definition in mind that Hexion's actions will be judged.

A.   Hexion's Failure to Use Reasonable Best Efforts to Consummate the Financing and Failure to Give Huntsman Notice of its Concerns

Hexion claims that it will be unable to consummate the merger because, if

---

[87]   A mistake of law is an excuse only if the mistake negates one of the elements of the offense. For example, if a law made it a felony to fail to report a crime, it would be a defense to such charge that the defendant was unaware the act he had witnessed was criminal. But it would not be a defense that he was unaware of his obligation to report crimes.

[89]   89 *See 24* WILLISTON ON CONTRACTS § 64:1 (4th ed.):
          The fundamental principle that underlies the availability of contract damages is that of compensation. That is, the disappointed promisee is generally entitled to an award of money damages in an amount reasonably calculated to make him or her whole and neither more nor less; any greater sum operates to punish the breaching promisor and results in an unwarranted windfall to the promisee, while any lesser sum rewards the promisor for his or her wrongful act in breaching the contract and fails to provide the promisee with the benefit of the bargain he or she made.

it were to do so, the resulting company would, according to Hexion, be insolvent. The commitment letter requires as a condition precedent to the banks' obligation to fund that the banks receive a solvency certificate or opinion indicating that the combined entity would be solvent.[93] Hexion argues that no qualified party will be able to deliver such an opinion in good faith, and as such the banks will be neither willing nor obligated to fund. Furthermore, Hexion claims, even if it were able to convince the banks to fund under the commitment letter, there would still be insufficient funds available to close the deal. Notably however, such was Apollo and Hexion's ardor for Huntsman in July 2007 that there is no "financing out" in this deal -- the conditions precedent to Hexion's obligation to close do not contain any requirement regarding the availability of the financing under the commitment letter. Nor is there a "solvency out," which would make Hexion's obligation to close contingent on the solvency of the combined entity. Nevertheless, as Apollo's desire for Huntsman cooled through the spring of 2008, Apollo and Hexion attempted to use the purported insolvency of the combined entity as an escape hatch to Hexion's obligations under the merger agreement.

Section 5.12(a) of the merger agreement contains Hexion's covenant to use its reasonable best efforts to consummate the financing:

> (a) [Hexion] shall use its reasonable best efforts to take, or cause to be taken, all actions and to do, or cause to be done, all things necessary, proper or advisable to arrange and consummate the Financing on the terms and conditions described in the Commitment Letter, including (I) using reasonable best efforts to (x) satisfy on a timely basis all terms, covenants and conditions set forth in the Commitment Letter; (y) enter into definitive agreements with respect thereto on the terms and conditions contemplated by the Commitment Letter; and (z) consummate the Financing at or prior to Closing; and (ii) seeking to enforce its rights under the Commitment Letter. Parent will furnish correct and complete copies of all such definitive agreements to the Company promptly upon their execution.

Put more simply, to the extent that an act was both commercially reasonable

---

[93]   PX 2 at D-2 P 6. Paragraph 6 of Exhibit D (which exhibit consists of additional conditions precedent to the banks' obligation to fund) reads in pertinent part:
> The [lending banks] shall have received (i) customary and reasonably satisfactory legal opinions, corporate documents and certificates (including a certificate from the chief financial officer of [Hexion] or the chief financial officer of [Huntsman] or an opinion from a reputable valuation firm with respect to solvency (on a consolidated basis) of the [combined company] and its subsidiaries on the Closing Date after giving effect to the Transactions) (all such opinions, documents and certificates mutually agreed to be in form and substance customary for recent financings of this type with portfolio companies controlled by affiliates of or funds managed by [Apollo]) ....

and advisable to enhance the likelihood of consummation of the financing, the onus was on Hexion to take that act. To the extent that Hexion deliberately chose not to act, but instead pursued another path designed to *avoid* the consummation of the financing, Hexion knowingly and intentionally breached this covenant.

Likewise, section 5.12(b) of the merger agreement provides in pertinent part:

> (b) [Hexion] shall keep the Company informed with respect to all material activity concerning the status of the Financing contemplated by the Commitment Letter and shall give [Huntsman] prompt notice of any material adverse change with respect to such Financing. Without limiting the foregoing, [Hexion] agrees to notify [Huntsman] promptly, and in any event within two Business Days, if at any time ... (iii) for any reason [Hexion] no longer believes in good faith that it will be able to obtain all or any portion of the Financing contemplated by the Commitment Letter on the terms described therein.

This provision is equally simple. Hexion covenants that it will let Huntsman know within two business days if it no longer believes in good faith it will be able to draw upon the commitment letter financing.

Sometime in May 2008, Hexion apparently became concerned that the combined entity, after giving effect to the merger agreement and the commitment letter, would be insolvent. At that time a reasonable response to such concerns might have been to approach Huntsman's management to discuss the issue and potential resolutions of it. This would be particularly productive to the extent that such potential insolvency problems rested on the insufficiency of operating liquidity, which could be addressed by a number of different "levers" available to management.[95] This is not what Hexion did. Instead Hexion, through Wachtell Lipton, engaged Duff & Phelps ostensibly to provide them guidance as to whether the combined entity would be in danger of being considered insolvent. At that point, Hexion's actions could not definitively be said to have been in breach of its obligations under section 5.12(a).

By early June, Duff & Phelps reported back to Wachtell Lipton and Hexion that, based on the information they had been provided, the combined company appeared to fail all three of the customary insolvency tests (the failure of any one of which is sufficient to render a company, for the purposes of delivering a solvency opinion, insolvent). By this point Hexion, assuming *arguendo* it believed in the projections it provided to Duff & Phelps in order to conduct the analysis, would have had a justifiable good faith concern that it would not be able to provide the required solvency certificate, and that the bank financing pursuant to the

---

[95] Both sides' management testified that there are many "levers" a corporate manager can "pull" to address operating liquidity concerns.

commitment letter might be imperiled. Hexion was then clearly obligated to approach Huntsman management to discuss the appropriate course to take to mitigate these concerns. Moreover, Hexion's obligations under the notification covenant in section 5.12(b) of the merger agreement was now in play. Because Hexion now had (again giving Hexion the benefit of the doubt) a good faith belief that the combined entity would be insolvent, Hexion had an absolute obligation to notify Huntsman of this concern within two days of coming to this conclusion, *i.e.* within two days of receiving Duff & Phelps's initial report.

But Hexion did nothing to approach Huntsman management, either to discuss ways the solvency problems might be addressed, or even to put Huntsman on notice of its concerns. This choice alone would be sufficient to find that Hexion had knowingly and intentionally breached its covenants under the merger agreement. Hexion in the days that followed would compound its breach further.

B.   Hexion Affirmatively Acts To Scuttle The Financing

Section 5.12(b) of the merger agreement contains more than an affirmative requirement that Hexion provide prompt notice to Huntsman if the financing is imperiled. It also contains a negative covenant:

> *[Hexion] shall not, and shall not* permit any of its Affiliates to, *without the prior written consent of [Huntsman], take or fail to take any action* or enter into any transaction, including any merger, acquisition, joint venture, disposition, lease, contract or debt or equity financing, *that could reasonably be expected to materially impair, delay or prevent consummation of the Financing contemplated by the Commitment Letter* or any Alternate Financing contemplated by any Alternate Financing. (emphasis added).

Hexion's obligation under the covenant here is again quite simple: do nothing without Huntsman's written consent which might reasonably be expected to scuttle or otherwise harm the likelihood or timing of the financing under the commitment letter.

Apparently considering Duff & Phelps's initial determination that the combined entity would likely be insolvent insufficient for its purposes, on June 2, 2008, Hexion engaged a second Duff & Phelps team headed by Wisler, to provide a formal solvency opinion, or, more to the point, a formal insolvency opinion.

The Duff & Phelps formal opinion team eventually delivered a formal insolvency opinion [97] to Hexion on June 18, 2008, which opinion was presented to the Hexion board the same day. Concluding that the board could rely on the opinion, Hexion's did not contact Huntsman to discuss the issue. If Hexion had contacted Huntsman at this point and requested a meeting between Hexion and Huntsman management to discuss strategies to address the apparent insolvency problem, Hexion would once again have been in compliance with its obligations under the covenants in sections 5.12(a) and (b), and any knowing and intentional breach resulting from its earlier failure to notify Huntsman would have been cured, as no prejudice to Huntsman would have occurred by Hexion's delay. But Hexion chose an alternative tack. Upon adopting the findings of the Duff & Phelps insolvency opinion on June 18, the Hexion board approved the filing of this lawsuit, and the initial complaint was filed that day. In that complaint, <u>Hexion publicly raised its claim that the combined entity would be insolvent, thus placing the commitment letter financing in serious peril.</u> The next day, June 19, 2008, Credit Suisse, the lead bank under the commitment letter, received a copy of the Duff & Phelps insolvency opinion from Hexion, all but killing any possibility that the banks would be willing to fund under the commitment letter. Morrison testified on cross-examination that he was well aware that this was virtually certain to be the consequence of delivering the insolvency opinion to the banks:

Q Okay. And it's correct that you sent the banks both a copy of this lawsuit complaint and a copy of the Duff & Phelps insolvency opinion. Correct?

A I believe so, yes.

Q And you carefully considered the consequences of your doing that, did you not?

A Yes.

Q Okay. You knew that providing this to the banks would make it virtually impossible for them to go forward with the financing?

A Yes.

Q Let's look back at the contract. You mentioned the contract. Again, JX 1. Let's look at 5.12(b). And let's go down toward the -- yes. Here we go. Right there. This is out of 5.12(b). Hexion, without the written consent of Huntsman, cannot take any action that would be reasonably expected to materially impair, delay or prevent the financing contemplated by the commitment letter. Correct?

A Yes.

Q And you are aware of this obligation. Correct? A Yes.

Q All right. And you didn't seek Huntsman's consent to deliver the Duff & Phelps insolvency opinion to the banks?

A No.

Q Right. And even though you knew that delivering that insolvency opinion would prevent consummation of the financing, you went ahead and did it, anyway?

A Yes.

 Given the court's conclusion that a "knowing and intentional" breach must be the deliberate commission of an act that constitutes a breach of a covenant in the merger agreement, Morrison's testimony makes clear that a knowing and intentional breach by Hexion had occurred by June 19, 2008.

Hexion offers two arguments to justify its taking such dramatic and irrevocable action. The first is that it wanted to secure its status as first filer in any lawsuit arising out of the contract in order to ensure for itself a Delaware forum for litigation. Although the merger agreement explicitly lays exclusive jurisdiction over such suits in the Delaware Court of Chancery, Zaken testified at trial that Apollo and Hexion were concerned that Huntsman might choose to bring suit in Texas instead. But this is clearly no defense to a claim that Hexion knowingly and intentionally breached its covenant not to act in any way which could be reasonably expected to harm the likelihood of the consummation of the financing without Huntsman's express written consent. This proposed defense amounts to nothing more than "we were afraid they might breach, so we breached first." Even if Huntsman had filed suit in Texas prior to Hexion's breach of section 5.12(b), to the extent that Huntsman's filing of a suit in Texas might not constitute a material breach of the merger agreement, Hexion's performance under the contract *still* would not be excused and it would have remained obligated to comply with the terms of the covenants under the merger agreement. [99] *A fortiori,* Hexion's obligation under the section 5.12(b) covenant cannot have been excused by Hexion's mere fear that Huntsman would breach the merger agreement by bringing suit in Texas. [The second argument is omitted. - Ed.]

* * *

V.

Huntsman asks the court to enter a judgment ordering Hexion and its merger subsidiary, Nimbus, to specifically perform their covenants and obligations under the merger agreement. For the reasons explained below, the court finds that, under the agreement, Huntsman cannot force Hexion to consummate the merger, but that Huntsman is entitled to a judgment ordering Hexion to specifically perform its other covenants and obligations.

The court first examines whether the merger agreement, somewhat unusually, contains a provision prohibiting the issuance of an order specifically directing Hexion to comply with its duty to close the transaction. Section 8.11 provides that generally a non-breaching party may seek and obtain specific performance of any covenant or obligation set forth in the agreement. However, that section goes on to state, in virtually impenetrable language, as follows: "In circumstances where [Hexion is] obligated to consummate the Merger and the Merger has not been consummated on or prior to the earlier of the last day of the Marketing Period or the Termination Date (other than as a result of [Huntsman's] refusal to close in violation of this Agreement) the parties acknowledge that [Huntsman] shall *not* be entitled to enforce specifically the obligations of [Hexion] to consummate the Merger."

Hexion argues that section 8.11 entirely precludes specific performance as a remedy for breach of its obligation to close. Andrew Nussbaum, a Wachtell Lipton partner advising Hexion during the negotiation and drafting of the merger agreement, testified that "[i]t was [Hexion's] position that we would agree to specific performance of our covenants under the agreement, with the exception of the obligation to close the merger." Nussbaum further testified that Huntsman accepted Hexion's position in the executed version of the agreement.

Huntsman did not question Nussbaum at trial regarding the parties' understanding of the specific performance section and did not offer contrary testimony by any of its lawyers. Instead, Huntsman attempts to undercut Nussbaum's testimony by arguing in its post-trial brief that the phrase "[i]n circumstances where ... [Huntsman] shall not be entitled to enforce specifically the obligation[] of [Hexion] to consummate the Merger" implies that some other circumstances must exist where specific performance of the obligation to close is available; otherwise, Huntsman argues, the drafters simply would have written "[u]nder no circumstances ... shall [Huntsman] be entitled to enforce specifically the obligations of [Hexion] to consummate the merger."[118] Huntsman then explains that the reason for the exception to its general right to demand specific performance was to protect the Marketing Period during which the lending banks were to syndicate the debt. Furthermore, Huntsman argues, the parties agreed that if the Marketing Period had passed or the Termination Date had arrived Huntsman *could* force Hexion to consummate the merger, as the lending banks would have had a chance to syndicate the debt. While Huntsman's argument makes commercial sense, the inartfully drafted provision does not say what Huntsman says it does.

The problem clause is the second condition to the carve-out from specific performance: if "the Merger has not been consummated on or prior to the earlier of the last day of the Marketing Period or the Termination Date," Huntsman cannot force Hexion to close. Literally the clause does not allow specific performance in any case where Huntsman could employ the remedy.[120]

---

[118]   Def's Post-Trial Br. 84. *See* 11 WILLISTON ON CONTRACTS § 32:5 (4th ed.) ("An interpretation which gives effect to all provisions of the contract is preferred to one which renders a portion of the writing superfluous, useless or inexplicable. A court will interpret a contract in a manner that gives reasonable meaning to all of its provisions, if possible.").

[120]   Assuming that the Marketing Period ends before the Termination Date, if the deal is not consummated on or before the end of the Marketing Period, the agreement does not allow specific performance of the obligation to close. The clause does not explicitly state whether specific performance is available *after* the Marketing Period and before the Termination Date. However, if the deal was still in need of specific performance, it follows that it *also* had not been consummated *prior* to the end of the Marketing Period -- and thus no specific performance is available. Specific performance would technically be available if the merger had already been consummated (on or prior to the earlier of the last day of the Marketing Period or the Termination Date), but at that point specific performance would be wholly unnecessary. Assuming that the Termination Date ends before the Marketing Period, on or before the end of the Termination Date specific performance of the obligation to close is not available. After the Termination Date, the agreement is terminated and specific performance would not be possible.

While generally Delaware courts attempt to interpret contracts in a manner that gives meaning to each provision, the meaning of the phrase at issue is unclear. When a provision is "fairly susceptible of different interpretations," as is the case here, "the court may consider extrinsic evidence." Here, Huntsman merely offers an unsupported argument about what the parties intended to mean, based on logic, but provides no evidence. In addition, Huntsman's argument contradicts how it explained the merger in the proxy statement it filed with the Security and Exchange Commission. On both pages 11 and 85, Huntsman reports:

> Each of the parties is specifically authorized to seek a decree or order of specific performance to enforce performance of any covenant or obligation under the merger agreement or injunctive relief to restrain any breach or threatened breach, provided that in a case where Hexion is obligated to close the merger, we may not specifically enforce its obligations to consummate the merger but only its obligations to cause its financing to be funded.

The proxy statement makes no mention of any circumstance under which Huntsman could specifically enforce Hexion's obligation to consummate the merger.

Nussbaum's uncontradicted testimony at trial coupled with the extrinsic evidence provided in Huntsman's own publicly filed proxy statement leads the court to find that the agreement does not allow Huntsman to specifically enforce Hexion's duty to consummate the merger. Instead, if all other conditions precedent to closing are met, Hexion will remain free to choose to refuse to close. Of course, if Hexion's refusal to close results in a breach of contract, it will remain liable to Huntsman in damages.

Turning to the remaining questions, there is no dispute that section 8.11 of the merger agreement reflects the parties' express agreement that irreparable injury would occur "in the event that any of the provisions of this Agreement were not performed in accordance with its specific terms or were otherwise breached." That same section also contains the parties' general agreement that, in the event of any breach, the non-breaching party shall be entitled to obtain an order of specific performance "to enforce the observance and performance of such covenant or obligation." Finally, section 8.11 provides that no party seeking an order of specific performance "shall be required to obtain, furnish or post any bond or similar instrument."

In view of these provisions, and considering all the circumstances, the court concludes that it is appropriate to require Hexion to specifically perform its obligations under the merger agreement, other than the obligation to close. Hexion does not argue otherwise. When it is known whether the financing contemplated by the commitment letter is available or not, Hexion and its shareholders will thus be placed in the position to make an informed judgment about whether to close the transaction (in light of, among other things, the findings and conclusions in this opinion) and, if so, how to finance the combined operations. As the parties recognize, both Hexion and Huntsman are solvent, profitable businesses. The issues in this case relate principally to the cost of the merger and whether the financing structure Apollo and Hexion arranged in July 2007 is adequate to close the deal and fund the operations of the combined enterprise. The order the court is today issuing will afford the parties the opportunity to resolve those issues in an orderly and sensible fashion.

VI.

For all the foregoing reasons, the court has today entered an Order and Final Judgment granting Huntsman Corporation relief in accordance with the findings of fact and conclusions of law set forth in this Opinion.

QUESTION:

1.   One commentator suggested that this case and IBP, among others, show that one who instigates the termination is the one that suffers. Could Hexion have achieved the desired result by taking other actions?

2.   Would Hexion have been better off just to terminate the agreement and tender the reverse termination fee, as Cerberus did when it terminated its agreement with United Rentals, described *supra* page 5?

The Aftermath

After this decision, Apollo added $540 million to Hexion's capital to try to overcome the insolvency issue. Not surprisingly, the banks refused to fund the loans, and Apollo brought suit against them. Huntsman settled with Hexion and Apollo for $1 billion. Huntsman continued its litigation against Credit Suisse and Deutsche Bank in Texas. Huntsman has argued that the banks conspired with Apollo and interfered with Huntsman's prior merger pact with previous suitor Basell. Huntsman will be able to ask the jury for funds its shareholders would have received had each deal gone through, or $3.6 billion for the Basell deal and $4.6 billion for the Hexion deal.

Insert in Chapter 6, Part 2A, at page 305, immediately before Note on Williams v. Geier:

Note on Gantler v. Stephens

Gantler v. Stephens, 965 A.2d 695 (Del. 2009), involved a shareholder suit against directors and officers of a small bank holding company in connection with a "going private" recapitalization. The board had first hired a financial adviser and explored the possibility of a sale.

"In December 2004, three potential purchasers -- Farmers National Banc Corp. ("Farmers"), Cortland Bancorp ("Cortland"), and First Place Financial Corp. ("First Place")--sent bid letters to Stephens. Farmers stated in its bid letter that it had no plans to retain the First Niles Board, and the Board did not further pursue the Farmers' offer. In its bid letter, Cortland offered $ 18 per First Niles share, 49% in cash and 51% in stock, representing a 3.4% premium over the current First Niles share price. Cortland also indicated that it would terminate all the incumbent Board members, but would consider them for future service on Cortland's board. First Place's bid letter, which made no representation regarding the continued retention of the First Niles Board, proposed a stock-for-stock transaction valued at $ 18 to $ 18.50 per First Niles Share, representing a 3.4% to 6.3% premium.

"The Board considered these bids at its next regularly scheduled meeting in December 2004. At that meeting the Financial Advisor opined that all three bids were within the range suggested by its financial models, and that accepting the stock-based offers would be superior to retaining First Niles shares. The Board took no action at that time. Thereafter, at that same meeting, Stephens also discussed in further detail Management's proposed privatization.

"On January 18, 2005, the Board directed the Financial Advisor and Management to conduct due diligence in connection with a possible transaction with First Place or Cortland. The Financial Advisor met with Stephens and Safarek, and all three reviewed Cortland's due diligence request. Stephens and Safarek agreed to provide the materials Cortland requested and scheduled a due diligence session for February 6. Cortland failed to receive the materials it requested, canceled the February 6 meeting, and demanded the submission of those materials by February 8. The due diligence materials were never furnished, and Cortland withdrew its bid for First Niles on February 10. Management did not inform the Board of these due diligence events until after Cortland had withdrawn its bid.

"First Place made its due diligence request on February 7, 2005, and asked for a due diligence review session the following week. Initially, Stephens did not provide the requested materials to First Place and resisted setting a date for a due diligence session. After Cortland withdrew its bid, however, Stephens agreed to schedule a due diligence session.

"First Place began its due diligence review on February 13, 2005, and submitted a revised offer to First Niles on March 4. As compared to its original offer, First Place's revised offer had an improved exchange ratio. Because of a decline in First Place's stock value, the revised offer represented a lower implied price per share ($ 17.25 per First Niles share), but since First Niles' stock price had also declined, the revised offer still represented an 11% premium over market price. The Financial Advisor opined that First Place's revised offer was within an acceptable range, and that it exceeded the mean and median comparable multiples for previous acquisitions involving similar banks.

"On March 7, 2005, at the next regularly scheduled Board meeting, Stephens informed the directors of First Place's revised offer. Although the Financial Advisor suggested that First Place might again increase the exchange ratio, the Board did not discuss the offer. Stephens proposed that the Board delay considering the offer until the next regularly scheduled Board meeting. After the Financial Advisor told him that First Place would likely not wait two weeks for a response, Stephens scheduled a special Board meeting for March 9 to discuss the First Place offer.

"On March 8, First Place increased the exchange ratio of its offer to provide an implied value of $ 17.37 per First Niles share. At the March 9 special Board meeting, Stephens distributed a memorandum from the Financial Advisor describing First Place's revised offer in positive terms. Without any discussion or deliberation, however, the Board voted 4 to 1 to reject that offer, with only Gander voting to accept it. After the vote, Stephens discussed Management's privatization plan and instructed Legal Counsel to further investigate that plan."

The Chancery Court had dismissed a complaint that the board breached its duties, and was reversed by the Supreme Court, en banc. Justice Jacobs, writing for the court stated:

"I.   The Court of Chancery Erroneously Dismissed Count I of the Complaint

"Count I of the complaint alleges that the defendants breached their duties of loyalty and care as directors and officers of First Niles by abandoning the Sales Process. Specifically, plaintiffs claim that the defendants improperly: (1) sabotaged the due diligence aspect of the Sales Process, (2) rejected the First Place offer, and (3) terminated the Sales Process, all for the purpose of retaining the benefits of continued incumbency.

"In his opinion, the Vice Chancellor concluded that *Unocal* did not apply, because the complaint did not allege any "defensive" action by the Board. The court also determined entire fairness review to be inappropriate, because (1) it would be problematic to determine "fair price" without a completed transaction, (2) the Board had not interposed itself between the shareholders and a potential acquirer by implementing defensive measures, and (3) entire fairness review would be inconsistent with the broad power allocated to directors.

"Accordingly, the Court of Chancery analyzed Count I under the business judgment standard, and concluded that the Count I allegations failed to rebut the presumption of business judgment. Because the Board had "initiated the Sales Process on its own accord, seemingly as a market check as part of an exploration of strategic alternatives[,]" that supported the Board's stated business purpose -- to reduce corporate expense associated with federal securities law compliance. The Vice Chancellor also concluded that the complaint failed to plead facts sufficient to infer disloyalty, and that given the Board's extensive discussions with, and receipt of reports from, the Financial Advisor, and given the involvement of specially retained Outside Counsel, the alleged facts were insufficient to establish a violation of the duty of care. The court therefore concluded that the challenged conduct was entitled to business judgment protection, which required the dismissal of Count I.

*   *   *

"On appeal, the plaintiffs claim that the legal sufficiency of Count I should have been determined under the heightened *Unocal* standard or, alternatively, under the entire fairness standard. Under either or both standards, plaintiffs urge, Count I would withstand a motion to dismiss. Additionally, plaintiffs argue that the dismissal of Safarek was error because a reasonable inference could be drawn that Safarek had actively sabotaged the due diligence process, thereby aiding and abetting Stephens' duty of loyalty violation.

"We conclude that the Court of Chancery erroneously dismissed Count I of the complaint for the reasons next discussed.

"**A.   The Court of Chancery Properly Refused to Apply Unocal Scrutiny**

"The plaintiffs first challenge the Vice Chancellor's determination that Count I was not subject to review under *Unocal*. We agree with that ruling and find no error. "Enhanced judicial scrutiny under *Unocal* applies 'whenever the record reflects that a board of directors took defensive measures in response to a perceived threat to corporate policy and effectiveness which touches on issues of control.'" [21] The plaintiffs argue that *Unocal* should apply because Count I alleges that the defendants rejected a value-maximizing bid in favor of a transaction that favored their self-interest at the shareholders' expense. Stated differently, plaintiffs argue that Count I, fairly read, alleges that the defendants stood to lose the benefits of corporate control if the Company were sold, and that they therefore took defensive action by sabotaging the due diligence process, rejecting the First Place offer, and terminating the Sales Process.   "The Court of Chancery properly refused to apply *Unocal* in this fashion. The premise of *Unocal* is "that the transaction at issue was defensive." [22] Count I sounds in disloyalty, not improper defensive conduct. Count

---

[21]   *In re Santa Fe Pac. Corp., S'holder Litig.*, 669 A.2d 59, 71 (Del. 1995) (quoting *Unitrin, Inc. v. Am. Gen. Corp.*, 651 A.2d 1361, 1372 n.9 (Del. 1995)).

[22]   *Shamrock Hldgs, Inc. v. Polaroid Corp.*, 559 A.2d 257, 271 (Del. Ch. 1989).

I does not allege any hostile takeover attempt or similar threatened external action from which it could reasonably be inferred that the defendants acted "defensively."

"B. The Court of Chancery Misapplied the Business Judgment Standard

"The plaintiffs next claim that the legal sufficiency of Count I should have been reviewed under the entire fairness standard. That claim is assessed within the framework of the business judgment standard, which is "a presumption that in making a business decision the directors of a corporation acted on an informed basis, in good faith and in the honest belief that the action taken was in the best interests of the company."

"Procedurally, the plaintiffs have the burden to plead facts sufficient to rebut that presumption. On a motion to dismiss, the pled facts must support a reasonable inference that in making the challenged decision, the board of directors breached either its duty of loyalty or its duty of care. If the plaintiff fails to satisfy that burden, "a court will not substitute its judgment for that of the board if the ... decision can be 'attributed to any rational business purpose.'"[27]

"We first consider the sufficiency of Count I as against the Director Defendants. That Count alleges that those defendants (together with non-party director Zuzolo) improperly rejected a value-maximizing bid from First Place and terminated the Sales Process. Plaintiffs allege that the defendants rejected the First Place bid to preserve personal benefits, including retaining their positions and pay as directors, as well as valuable outside business opportunities. The complaint further alleges that the Board failed to deliberate before deciding to reject the First Place bid and to terminate the Sales Process. Indeed, plaintiffs emphasize, the Board retained the Financial Advisor to advise it on the Sales Process, yet repeatedly disregarded the Financial Advisor's advice.

"A board's decision not to pursue a merger opportunity is normally reviewed within the traditional business judgment framework. In that context the board is entitled to a strong presumption in its favor, because implicit in the board's statutory authority to propose a merger, is also the power to decline to do so.

"Our analysis of whether the Board's termination of the Sales Process merits the business judgment presumption is two pronged. First, did the Board reach its decision in the good faith pursuit of a legitimate corporate interest? Second, did the Board do so advisedly? For the Board's decision here to be entitled to the business judgment presumption, both questions must be answered affirmatively.

"We consider first whether Count I alleges a cognizable claim that the Board breached its duty of loyalty. In *TW Services v. SWT Acquisition Corporation*, the Court of Chancery recognized that a board's decision to decline a merger is often

---

[27] *Shamrock Hldgs, Inc. v. Polaroid Corp.*, 559 A.2d 257, 271 (Del. Ch. 1989).

rooted in distinctively corporate concerns, such as enhancing the corporation's long term share value, or "a plausible concern that the level of debt likely to be borne by [the target company] following any merger would be detrimental to the long term function of th[at] [c]ompany." A good faith pursuit of legitimate concerns of this kind will satisfy the first prong of the analysis.[31]

"Here, the plaintiffs allege that the Director Defendants had a disqualifying self-interest because they were financially motivated to maintain the status quo. A claim of this kind must be viewed with caution, because to argue that directors have an entrenchment motive solely because they could lose their positions following an acquisition is, to an extent, tautological. By its very nature, a board decision to reject a merger proposal could always enable a plaintiff to assert that a majority of the directors had an entrenchment motive. For that reason, the plaintiffs must plead, in addition to a motive to retain corporate control, other facts sufficient to state a cognizable claim that the Director Defendants acted disloyally.[32]

"The plaintiffs have done that here. At the time the Sales Process was terminated, the Board members were Stephens, Kramer, Eddy, Zuzolo and Gander. Only Gander voted to accept the First Place merger bid. The pled facts are sufficient to establish disloyalty of at least three (*i.e.*, a majority) of the remaining directors, which suffices to rebut the business judgment presumption. First, the Reclassification Proxy itself admits that the Company's directors and officers had "a conflict of interest with respect to [the Reclassification] because he or she is in a position to structure it in a way that benefits his or her interests differently from the interest of the unaffiliated stockholders." Second, a director-specific analysis establishes (for Rule 12(b)(6) purposes) that a majority of the Board was conflicted.

"Stephens: Aside from Stephens losing his long held positions as President, Chairman and CEO of First Niles and the Bank, the plaintiffs have alleged specific conduct from which a duty of loyalty violation can reasonably be inferred. Stephens never responded to Cortland's due diligence request. The Financial Advisor noted that Stephens' failure to respond had caused Cortland to withdraw its bid. Even after Cortland had offered First Niles an extension, Stephens did not furnish the necessary due diligence materials, nor did he inform the Board of these due diligence problems until after Cortland withdrew. Cortland had also explicitly stated in its bid letter that the incumbent Board would be terminated if Cortland acquired

---

[31]   1989 Del. Ch. LEXIS 19, [WL] at *11.

[32]   See Pogostin v. Rice, 480 A.2d 619, 627 (Del. 1984), *overruled on other grounds by Brehm v. Eisner*, 746 A.2d 244 (Del. 2000) ("plaintiffs have failed to plead any facts supporting their claim[s] that the ... board rejected the ... offer solely to retain control. Rather, plaintiffs seek to establish a motive or primary purpose to retain control only by showing that the ... board opposed a tender offer. Acceptance of such an argument would condemn any board, which successfully avoided a takeover, regardless of whether that board properly determined that it was acting in the best interests of the shareholders.").

First Niles. From these alleged facts it may reasonably be inferred that what motivated Stephens' unexplained failure to respond promptly to Cortland's due diligence request was his personal financial interest, as opposed to the interests of the shareholders. That same inference can be drawn from Stephens' response to the First Place bid: Count I alleges that Stephens attempted to "sabotage" the First Place due diligence request in a manner similar to what occurred with Cortland.

"Thus, the pled facts provide a sufficient basis to conclude, for purposes of a Rule 12(b)(6) motion to dismiss, that Stephens acted disloyally.

* * *

"In summary, the plaintiffs have alleged facts sufficient to establish, for purposes of a motion to dismiss, that a majority of the First Niles Board acted disloyally. Because a cognizable claim of disloyalty rebuts the business judgment presumption, we need not reach the separate question of whether, in deciding to terminate the Sales Process, the Director Defendants acted advisedly (*i.e.*, with due care). Because the claim of disloyalty was subject to entire fairness review, the Court of Chancery erred in dismissing Count I as to the Director Defendants on the basis of the business judgment presumption.[1]"

Insert in Chapter 6, Part 2B, at page 326, after *Campbell v. Potash Company of Saskatchewan*:

Note: Shareholder Activism, Compensation Policies and Golden Parachutes

In the past few years activist investors have been campaigning for a shareholder voice in executive compensation. One form of that has involved severance arrangements. Many shareholder proposals, under Rule 14a-8 urge

---

[1]   The Court of Chancery determined that entire fairness review was inappropriate, because: (1) it would be problematic to determine "fair price" without a completed transaction, (2) the Board did not interpose itself between the shareholders and a potential acquirer by implementing any defensive measures, and (3) entire fairness review would be inconsistent with Delaware's broad allocation to power to directors. *See Gander v. Stephens*, 2008 Del. Ch. LEXIS 20, 2008 WL 401124, at *9-10 (Del. Ch. February 14, 2008). Although it may be problematic to determine the fair price of a transaction that was never finalized, our decisions have applied the entire fairness standard in a non-transaction context. *See Nixon v. Blackwell*, 626 A.2d 1366, 1376 (Del. 1993) (applying the fair dealing prong of entire fairness). That the Board did not implement any impermissible defensive measures does not, *ipso facto*, insulate their actions from entire fairness review. Nor does Delaware's broad allocation of power to directors require less searching review where shareholders are able to establish a cognizable claim of self-interested director behavior.

policies that limit such payments. There are current proposals to allow delivery of proxies by e-mail, which will further lower the costs of such proposals for activist investors. Under Rule 14a-8 shareholders can request that management adopt certain policies, but where they involve the management of the business, shareholders lack power under corporate statutes to take such actions unilaterally.

Typically shareholder proposals will recommend a policy that caps severance payments, either at two or three times annual compensation. Many of these shareholder proposals are quite brief, and companies that adopt them in the recommended form may well encounter interpretation difficulties. Many severance arrangements involve payments in excess of three times the average annual compensation of an executive who departs after a change of control. As a result, they trigger a 20% excise tax for the receiving executive, in addition to the normal income tax liability. In order to make these "excess parachute payments" similar to those below the threshold, many companies have committed to gross up the payments, with an additional amount necessary to cover the excise tax (plus the additional excise tax generated by the gross-up). Are these gross-ups "benefits" within the meaning of the policy? Typically these policies do not address this issue.

Another area of ambiguity involves payments already earned by but not yet paid to the executive, such as deferred compensation. Some policies exclude these payments from the definition of severance benefits. Where an executive has a bonus agreement, is that part of the severance payments in the year where the executive is paid a pro rata part of his or her earned bonus? Or should it count against average compensation for the measuring period? In some cases executives may be entitled to earn long-term incentives, in the form of shares of the target company. Typically these awards will be for multiple years, with a portion vesting each year. What happens if vesting is accelerated in the year of the change of control? All of these questions create litigation risk for any board interpreting these potentially ambiguous provisions. Hewlett-Packard has been the subject of a shareholder class action for its payments in connection with the removal of Carly Fiorina as CEO in 2005.

One of the problems with a policy that requires shareholder approval is its rigidity. Where a company is in negotiations to hire an outside executive who insists on a severance agreement in excess of policy limits, the company may be unable to grant this request without shareholder approval. Ordinarily a company will not have the time to call a special shareholders' meeting to grant an exception or to amend the policy. In 2005 Cendant Corporation declined to implement a golden parachute policy despite support from 65% of the shares voted at its 2005 annual meeting, stating:

> Our board has determined that if it changed our policy to the proposed policy ... we could be put at a competitive disadvantage because, among other things, the proposal would create uncertainty and delay in finalizing severance arrangements until after the arrangement is approved by our

stockholders, which could hinder our flexibility to attract, motivate and retain the best executive talent in today's competitive environment and in the future.

―――――――――――

Insert on page 345, after QUESTIONS:

NOTE ON MERCIER V. INTER-TEL, INCORPORATED

Mercier v. Inter-Tel, Incorporated, 929 A.2d 786 (Del. Ch. 2007) illustrates that Blasius is most concerned with director accountability and proxy fights for control of board seats. Vice Chancellor Strine summarized his opinion as follows:

> In this decision based on a preliminary injunction record, I conclude that well-motivated, independent directors may reschedule an imminent special meeting at which the stockholders are to consider an all cash, all shares offer from a third-party acquiror when the directors: (1) believe that the merger is in the best interests of the stockholders; (2) know that if the meeting proceeds the stockholders will vote down the merger; (3) reasonably fear that in the wake of the merger's rejection, the acquiror will walk away from the deal and the corporation's stock price will plummet; (4) want more time to communicate with and provide information to the stockholders before the stockholders vote on the merger and risk the irrevocable loss of the pending offer; and (5) reschedule the meeting within a reasonable time period and do not preclude or coerce the stockholders from freely deciding to reject the merger.

929 A.2d at 787-788.

―――――――――――

Insert in Chapter 6, page 351 at the end of Note on Federal Law Concerning Defenses to Proxy Fights:

Judicial interpretation of these bylaws in Delaware has been hostile to attempts to block shareholder proposals. In Jana Master Fund, Ltd. v. CNET Networks, Inc., 2008 Del. Ch. 35, affirmed May 13, 2008,, CNET's advance notice bylaw, Article II, §3, provided as follows:

> Any stockholder of the Corporation that has been the beneficial owner of at least $1,000 of securities entitled to vote at an annual meeting for at least one year *may seek to transact other corporate business* at the annual meeting, provided that such business is set forth in a written notice and mailed by certified mail to the Secretary of the Corporation and received no later than 120 calendar days in advance of the date of the Corporation's proxy statement released to security-holders in connection with the previous year's annual meeting of security holders (or, if no annual

meeting was held in the previous year or the date of the annual meeting has been changed by more than 30 calendar days from the date contemplated at the time of the previous year's proxy statement, a reasonable time before the solicitation is made). *Notwithstanding the foregoing, such notice must also comply with any applicable federal securities laws establishing the circumstances under which the Corporation is required to include the proposal in its proxy statement or form of proxy.* [Emphasis added.]

JANA sought to solicit proxies to replace two incumbent directors, expand the board from eight to thirteen and nominate five candidates to fill the new directorships, which would give it a majority on the board. JANA wrote CNET notifying it of JANA's intent to solicit proxies for these purposes, and requested inspection of a shareholder list under section 220 of the Del. GCL. CNET refused, arguing that JANA failed to state a proper purpose because its request was not timely under the advance notice bylaw. Chancellor Chandler held that the bylaw was not applicable to JANA's proposal, which was to solicit its own proxies, because the bylaw only applied to requests to have a shareholder's proposals included in the company's proxy under Rule 14a-8 of the Exchange Act. He summarized his holding:

> The language of the Notice Bylaw leads to only one reasonable conclusion: the bylaw applies solely to proposals and nominations that are intended to be included in the company's proxy materials pursuant to Rule 14a-8. One may parse the bylaw as follows: (1) notice of CNET's annual meeting will be provided to stockholders sometime between ten and sixty days before the meeting is held; (2) any stockholder who has owned $1,000 of stock for at least a year before the meeting may seek to transact other corporate business at the meeting; (3) to do so, that stockholder must send the CNET secretary notice of what business he/she plans to conduct a certain number of days before CNET needs to send out its proxy materials; and, finally, (4) in addition, such notice must also comply with the federal securities laws governing shareholder proposals a corporation must include in its own proxy materials. There are three related reasons I conclude this bylaw can be read only to apply to proposals under Rule 14a-8. First, the notion that a stockholder "may seek to transact other corporate business" does not make sense outside the context of Rule 14a-8. Second, it is reasonable to conclude this bylaw applies only to proposals shareholders want included on management's proxy materials because the bylaw sets the deadline for notice specifically in advance of the release of management's proxy form. Third, and most importantly, the explicit language of the final sentence makes clear that the scope of the bylaw is limited to proposals and nominations a shareholder wishes to have included on management's form of proxy.

A similar result was reached by Vice Chancellor Noble in Levitt Corp. v. Office Depot, Inc., 2008 Del. Ch. LEXIS 47 one month after the JANA decision.

Here Levitt sought to nominate two candidates for election to Office Depot's board. Levitt filed its own proxy statement soliciting proxies, but did not give notice under Office Depot's advance notice bylaw. Office Depot took the position that Levitt's nominations could not properly be brought before the meeting, and Levitt brought suit and won. The bylaw read as follows:

> Section 14. Stockholder Proposals. At an annual meeting of the stockholders, only such business shall be conducted as shall have been properly brought before the meeting. To be properly brought before an annual meeting, business must be (I) specified in the notice of the meeting (or any supplement thereto) given by or at the direction of the Board of Directors, (ii) otherwise properly brought before the meeting by or at the direction of the Board of Directors or (iii) otherwise properly brought before the meeting by a stockholder of the corporation who was a stockholder of record at the time of giving of notice provided for in this Section, who is entitled to vote at the meeting and who complied with the notice procedures set forth in this Section. For business to be properly brought before an annual meeting by a stockholder, the stockholder must have given timely notice thereof in writing to the Secretary . . . .

> To be timely, a stockholder's notice shall be received at the company's principal office . . ., not less than 120 calendar days before the date of Company's proxy statement released to shareholders in connection with the previous year's annual meeting. . . .

> Such stockholder's notice shall set forth as to each matter the stockholder proposes to bring before the annual meeting (I) a brief description of the business desired to be brought before the meeting and the reasons for conducting such business at the meeting and any material interest in such business of such stockholder and the beneficial owner, if any, on whose behalf the proposal is made; and (ii) as to the stockholder giving the notice and the beneficial owner, if any, on whose behalf the proposal is made (A) the name and address of such stockholder . . . , (B) the class and number of shares of the corporation which are owned of record and beneficially . . . , and (iii) in the event that such business includes a proposal to amend either the Articles of Incorporation or the Bylaws of the corporation, the language of the proposed amendment. . . . .

> Nothing in these Bylaws shall be deemed to affect any rights of the stockholders to request inclusion of proposals in the corporation's proxy statement pursuant to Rule 14a-8 under the Exchange Act.

Vice Chancellor Noble held that the election of directors was covered by the term "business" in the first sentence of the bylaw, despite the absence of a specific reference to nominations and elections of directors. Second, he held that nomination of directors was covered by the bylaw, as the nomination is an essential part of the election process. But he then held that notice had been given by Home Depot that satisfied these requirements as the election of directors was mentioned as a subject for action in Office Depot's own notice of the meeting.

PROBLEM

What changes would you make to Office Depot's bylaws to make them more restrictive?

Insert at beginning of Note on page 381:

Selectica, Inc. v. Versata Enterprises, Inc., 2010 Del. Ch. LEXIS 39, involved the use of a poison pill not to prevent a takeover (although it would have that effect if left in place) but to prevent an "ownership change" within the meaning of section 382 of the Internal Revenue Code, dealing with net operating loss ("NOL") carryforwards. Selectica had operated at a loss since it became a public company in 2000, and had, according to one opinion, approximately $165 million NOLs, which could be carried forward as an offset against future taxable income for up to twenty years. The Treasury has always been concerned that companies might attempt to "traffic" in NOLs, and use them to reduce taxes for unrelated businesses. Section 382 of the IRC imposes limitations on their use after an "ownership change," which occurs when more than 50% of a firm's stock ownership changes over a three-year period. Since many companies' shares are widely held and trade regularly, this rule is limited to those who have held, during the relevant three-year period, 5% or more of the company's stock. Steel Partners, a private equity fund, had held 14.9% of Selectica's stock, and a competitor and potential buyer, Versata, held approximately 6.1%. A 2006 study showed that prior changes in ownership had cost Selectica $24.6 million in forfeited NOLs. By November of 2008 cumulative acquisitions by 5% shareholders had reached 40%, putting Selectica close to another "ownership change" that would forfeit more NOLs. By February 2009 at least half a dozen prospects had offered letters of intent, and by April Selectica had entered into exclusive negotiations with a potential buyer.

During this period Versata had been engaged in litigation with Selectica and offered to settle by purchasing Selectica for prices the Selectica board rejected. At the same time Steel Partners was urging a sale that would realize the value of Selectica's NOLs. Selectica had adopted a standard poison pill, which would be triggered at the 15% ownership level. The board was advised that its NOLs were a significant asset that was at risk if present or future 5% shareholders acquired another 10% of its stock. There after the board amended its poison pill to decrease the triggering ownership amount to 5%, while grandfathering existing 5% shareholders and permitting them to purchase modest increments. Trilogy, Inc., the parent of Versata, purchased additional shares to reach 6.7% ownership, and thus triggered the rights plan. The rights plan allowed Selectica's board to declare Trilogy an "exempt person" during the 10-days following the trigger, upon its determination that Trilogy would not jeopardize the NOLs. When Trilogy refused to sign a stand-still agreement, the board let the rights be triggered. The rights plan allowed the board to satisfy the rights by exchanging each right for one new share of common stock (excluding Trilogy), which it did. At the same time the board adopted a new 5% pill (the "Reloaded NOL Pill"). Selectica sought a declaratory judgment that its actions were valid and proper.

Trilogy challenged the board's adoption of a 5% pill as unrelated to a threat to Selectica, largely on the ground that the NOLs were of uncertain value, since no one could know whether Selectica would have any earnings, much less a large amount that could be offset by the NOLs. Because several of the directors were holding office temporarily, the court held that the board did not meet the requirements for "material enhancement" of deference under Unocal. But the court held that a threat to the NOLs met the test for a threat to a threat to a corporate objective. The court noted the growing number of 5% triggers in pills designed to protect NOLs. The court was not persuaded by the indeterminate value of the NOLs that they were not worth protecting.

Turning to the reasonableness of the response to the perceived threat, the court noted that a typical pill with a 15% trigger is not regarded as preclusive or coercive, noting that Moran v. Household International held that pills do not affect the right of stockholders to receive tender offers or restrict proxy contests. The court rejected Trilogy's argument that restricting ownership to 4.9% made a proxy contest impossible, because holding a large block was essential to credibility in a proxy fight. The court noted evidence that challengers with ownership in that range had succeeded in gaining board seats at a number of proxy contests in micro-cap companies such as Selectica. The court set a high standard for preclusion: "either the mathematical impossibility or realistic unattainability of a proxy contest...." The court found that the board had evaluated the potential consequences of adoption, including discouragement of institutional investors, prevention of 5% shareholders selling their shares as a single block, and discouragement of takeovers, and satisfied its Unocal obligations. These rulings applied to both the amendment of the original pill and the adoption of the subsequent Reloaded NOL Pill.

Substitute the following for Barkan v. Amsted Industries at page 560:

In Re NYMEX Shareholder Litigation

2009 Del. Ch. LEXIS 176

NOBLE, Vice Chancellor

pro

These two actions involved challenges to the now-consummated acquisition of Defendant NYMEX Holdings, Inc. ("NYMEX") by an entity controlled by Defendant CME Group, Inc. ("CME"). Some of the claims are brought on behalf of former shareholders of NYMEX. Others are brought on behalf of the Class A Members (i.e., those "seat holders" having contractual trading rights) of the NYMEX Exchange, which was a subsidiary of NYMEX.

In this memorandum opinion, the Court addresses Defendants' motions to dismiss both actions.

I. BACKGROUND

A. *The Parties*

NYMEX (or the "Company"), formerly a publicly traded Delaware corporation, was the largest commodity futures exchange in the world. The Company's principal operations were conducted through its two subsidiaries, the New York Mercantile Exchange, Inc. ("NYMEX Exchange") and Commodity Exchange, Inc. ("COMEX").

Plaintiffs Cataldo Capozza, Polly Winters, and Joan Haedrich owned NYMEX common stock. * * *

Defendant Richard Schaeffer was the chairman of both NYMEX and NYMEX Exchange and was a member of the NYMEX Board of Directors (the "Board"). Schaeffer also had been a Class A Member of the NYMEX Exchange since 1981. Defendant James Newsome was the President, Chief Executive Officer, and a member of the Board of Directors of NYMEX. In addition to Schaeffer and Newsome, all of the other members of the Board are named as individual Defendants (the "Director Defendants"). [10]

Defendant CME formed Defendant CMEG NY, Inc. as its wholly-owned subsidiary for the purpose of acquiring NYMEX.

B. Pre-Merger Modifications to NYMEX's Structure

From 1872 until 2000, NYMEX Exchange operated as a New York not-for-profit membership organization. [When it demutualized the former members of the Exchange became stockholders as well as "Class A Members" with certain contract rights that were also subject to this litigation.]

C. The Merger

In July 2007, the Board established the Strategic Initiatives Committee (the "SIC") in order to consider, negotiate, and recommend any significant transactions involving the Company. In or about June or July 2007, John Thain ("Thain"), then Chairman of the New York Stock Exchange ("NYSE"), met with Schaeffer and expressed NYSE's interest in acquiring NYMEX. As discussions progressed, Thain, on behalf on NYSE, spoke of purchasing NYMEX for $ 142 per share, reflecting a meaningful premium above the trading price. NYSE ultimately did not make a formal offer to purchase NYMEX. The Complaint alleges that Schaeffer did not inform the SIC or the Board of either his communications with Thain or NYSE's interest in purchasing NYMEX for $ 142 per share. It further alleges that "NYSE ultimately declined to make a formal proposal for purchasing NYMEX because Schaeffer personally demanded a senior executive position for himself as a pre-condition to the deal."

Sometime in late spring 2007, Schaeffer and Newsome began negotiating the sale of NYMEX to CME with Terry Duffy, CME's Chairman, and Craig Donahue, CME's Chief Executive Officer, but, it is alleged, they did not provide the Board or the SIC any of the details of these negotiations. The Board, however, was made aware that negotiations between the two companies were in progress for the purpose of a business combination. On January 7, 2008, NYMEX and CME entered into a confidentiality agreement in order to discuss more fully a potential acquisition. On January 9, 2008, the Board approved the adoption of a change of control severance plan, "which provide[d] for more than $ 97 million in change in control payments to senior management."[19] [19]

On January 28, 2008, NYMEX announced that it was in the process of negotiating a potential combination with CME, and that CME had offered to buy NYMEX for approximately $ 119 per share, which represented a 2.1% premium over the closing price of NYMEX shares on that day and an 11% premium above the closing price of NYMEX shares on the last trading day prior to the announcement. A substantial portion of the merger consideration was to be paid in CME stock. The Company also announced that it had entered into a 30-day exclusive negotiating period with CME. The Complaint alleges that, prior to any formal agreement between CME and NYMEX, "Schaeffer and Newsome committed to Duffy and Donahue that NYMEX would not attempt to renegotiate any of the economic terms of the proposed sale," and that this alleged arrangement was not disclosed to the Board.

On January 24, 2008, only four days before NYMEX announced that it was in exclusive merger discussions with CME, CME stock had closed at $ 635.14 per share, an almost $ 90 per share increase over its closing price a week earlier. The Complaint alleges that NYMEX timed the announcement of the exclusivity period in order for CME to capitalize on the recent increase in its stock price. One week after the announcement, however, CME stock fell to $ 485.25 per share. The CME offer did not contain a "collar"--a mechanism that could have offered some protection against market fluctuations in CME stock--on the stock portion of the merger consideration. Accordingly, because a substantial portion of the consideration in CME's offer was CME stock, the loss in value of CME stock had the effect of materially reducing the total merger consideration.

---

[19]   NYMEX's Compensation Committee first discussed the severance plan on November 19, 2007, and voted to recommend it to the NYMEX Board on December 11, 2007. In July 2008, the Board reduced the overall cost of the severance plan to $ 67 million.

The Complaint alleges that CME offered to "collar" the stock portion of the merger consideration, but such offer was rejected by Schaeffer and Newsome because it would have adversely affected the value of their NYMEX stock options. Accordingly, Schaeffer and Newsome did not inform the board that CME had offered a collar.

Despite the decline in the price of CME stock, the parties extended the 30-day exclusivity period to March 15, 2008. On March 17, 2008, NYMEX announced that it had entered into a merger agreement with CME. Pursuant to the merger agreement, which was unchanged from the terms of CME's original offer, CME was to acquire all of NYMEX's common stock in exchange for $ 36 per share in cash and 0.1323 shares of CME common stock per NYMEX share. However, based upon the value of CME stock before the capital markets' opening on March 17, 2008, the implied value of the merger consideration had declined to $ 100.30 per NYMEX share. The Complaint alleges that the Board approved the transaction "without obtaining, soliciting, or attempting to solicit other, higher bids for the Company's shares."

On or about March 16, 2008, the Board obtained fairness opinions on the acquisition from J.P. Morgan Securities, Inc. ("J.P. Morgan") and Merrill Lynch, Pierce, Fenner & Smith Incorporated ("Merrill Lynch"). Both financial advisors opined that the consideration to be paid to NYMEX shareholders was fair as of the date the fairness opinions were issued. The Complaint alleges that the discounted cash flow analyses performed by both financial advisors were flawed, which resulted in an improperly low implied range of values for NYMEX stock.

*   *   *

The Board unanimously approved the merger. In addition, over 95% of the shares voted were voted in favor of the merger.   *   *   * The merger was consummated on August 22, 2008.

D.   Shareholder Class Allegations

In the NYMEX Action, the shareholder class plaintiffs allege numerous breaches by Defendants of the fiduciary duties of loyalty, due care and candor in the sale of NYMEX to CME, and that, as a result of such breaches, NYMEX shareholders did not receive fair value for their shares. Plaintiffs allege that the Board is controlled by Chairman Richard Schaeffer, and that the Board agreed to sell NYMEX through an unfair process at an inadequate price in order for Schaeffer and NYMEX Chief Executive Officer and President James Newsome to obtain nearly $ 60 million in severance payments.[41] Plaintiffs point to Schaeffer's alleged

---

[41]   Of the original $ 96 million in executive severance payments, Schaeffer would receive $ 35 million and Newsome would receive $ 24 million if they were terminated "without cause" or resigned for "good reason" during the eighteen months following the change in control.

scuttling of a more favorable deal with NYSE, his behavior with respect to certain, unrelated transactions involving the Board, as well as his central role in the CME negotiations as evidence that he "rule[d] the Board with an iron hand." The fiduciary duty breaches committed by the Board, it is alleged, include omitting or misstating necessary information in NYMEX's proxy statements with respect to the CME deal, agreeing to CME's first and only offer, failing to inquire into other potential transactions, agreeing to a 30-day exclusive negotiating period with CME, allegedly causing investment bankers to understate the value of NYMEX shares in fairness opinions supporting the transaction, and agreeing to a $ 50 million breakup fee. In addition, Plaintiffs assert that the Board breached its fiduciary duties by agreeing to the $ 97 million change in control plan with an acquisition agreement imminent. The shareholder Plaintiffs further assert specific breaches of fiduciary duties by Defendants Schaeffer and Newsome in the context of their roles in negotiating the CME transaction, as well as by Schaeffer in his dealings with NYSE in the summer of 2007. Finally, Plaintiffs assert that the CME Defendants aided and abetted the NYMEX Defendants in the breach of these duties.

*   *   *

II.   ANALYSIS

*   *   *

B.   The NYMEX Action

Count I of the Complaint alleges that Schaeffer, Newsome, and the Board breached their fiduciary duties of care and loyalty. Count II of the Complaint alleges that the CME Defendants aided and abetted those alleged breaches.

1.   Substantive Claims Against the NYMEX Defendants

The Plaintiffs contend that various fiduciary failures by the Defendant Directors resulted in an unfair price obtained through an unfair process.

The parties dispute whether this case should be evaluated under Revlon, Inc. v. MacAndrews & Forbes Holdings, Inc. as involving a fundamental change of corporate control or whether it should be evaluated under the business judgment rule, which may be viewed as granting greater deference to board action.[48] The parties agree--as they must--that Revlon scrutiny applies only to transactions "'in

---

[48]   See, e.g., Moran v. Household Int'l, Inc., 500 A.2d 1346, 1356 (Del. 1985) ("The business judgment rule is a presumption that in making a business decision the directors of a corporation acted on an informed basis, in good faith and in the honest belief that the action taken was in the best interests of the company." (internal quotation marks omitted)); 1 Stephen A. Radin, The Business Judgment Rule: Fiduciary Duties for Corporate Directors 11-15 (6th ed. 2009).

which a fundamental change of corporate control occurs or is contemplated.'"[49] They dispute what constitutes a fundamental change of control sufficient to trigger Revlon scrutiny. A fundamental change of control does not occur for purposes of Revlon where control of the corporation remains, post-merger, in a large, fluid market. [50] Thus, for example, in a transaction where cash is the exclusive consideration paid to the acquired corporation's shareholders, a fundamental change of corporate control occurs--thereby triggering Revlon--because control of the corporation does not continue in a large, fluid market. In transactions, such as the present one, that involve merger consideration that is a mix of cash and stock--the stock portion being stock of an acquirer whose shares are held in a large, fluid market--"[t]he [Delaware] Supreme Court has not set out a black line rule explaining what percentage of the consideration can be cash without triggering Revlon."[51] In In re Santa Fe Pacific Corp. Shareholder Litigation, the Supreme Court held that a merger transaction involving consideration of 33% cash and 67% stock did not trigger Revlon.[52] In contrast, in Lukens, this Court stated that a merger transaction involving consideration of 60% cash and 40% stock likely triggered Revlon.[53] Here, the consideration paid to NYMEX shareholders was 56% CME stock and 44% cash, falling between the standards of Santa Fe and Lukens.[54] The parties therefore argue over whether Revlon has been triggered.[55]

The Court, however, need not decide whether Revlon scrutiny applies to the present transaction. NYMEX's Certificate of Incorporation contains an exculpatory clause authorized by 8 Del. C. § 102(b)(7) that protects the NYMEX directors from personal monetary liability for breaches of the duty of care. Thus, even if Revlon applied to this case, application of the exculpatory clause would lead to dismissal unless the Plaintiffs have successfully pleaded a failure to act loyally (or in good faith), which would preclude reliance on the Section 102(b)(7) provision.[56] For the

---

[49]   Paramount Commc'ns Inc. v. QVC Network Inc., 637 A.2d 34, 46 (Del. 1994) (quoting Barkan v. Amsted Indus., Inc., 567 A.2d 1279, 1286 (Del. 1989)).

[51]   In re Lukens Inc. S'holders Litig., 757 A.2d at 732, n. 25.

[52]   669 A.2d 59, 64, 70-71 (Del. 1995).

[53]   In re Lukens, Inc. S'holders Litig., 757 A.2d at 732 n.25.

[54]   At the time that the Board approved the transaction, the cash component comprised 36% of the total consideration, while CME stock made up 64%.

[55]   Plaintiffs also assert that the fact that the severance plan treats the transaction as a change in control additionally mandates that Revlon's scrutiny be applied (citing to Louisiana Mun. Police Employees' Ret. Sys. v. Crawford, 918 A.2d at 1172, 1179 n.6 (Del. Ch. 2007)).

[56]   See Lyondell Chemical Co. v. Ryan, 970 A.2d 235, 239 (Del. 2009) (noting that because "Lyondell's charter include[d] an exculpatory provision, pursuant to 8 Del. C. § 102(b)(7), . . . th[e] case turn[ed] on whether any arguable shortcomings on the part of the Lyondell directors also implicate[d] their duty of loyalty, a breach of which is not

reasons set forth below, they have not. Accordingly, the motion to dismiss the shareholders' substantive merger claims for failure to state a breach of fiduciary duty claim must be granted.

The Plaintiffs argue that that they have sufficiently alleged that Schaeffer, Newsome, and the Board acted disloyally. At the outset, the Court observes that the Plaintiffs must plead sufficient facts to show that a majority of the Board of Directors breached the fiduciary duty of loyalty; whether they otherwise would have stated a claim against Schaeffer and Newsome would not be controlling. That two directors may have been conflicted does not, by itself, impinge upon the independence of the remaining members of the Board--all of whom supported the merger. Accordingly, the Court addresses the Board's alleged breach of the duty of loyalty.

In order to state a claim for breach of the duty of loyalty, the Plaintiffs must plead facts from which this Court can reasonably infer that either: "a majority of the Director Defendants either stood on both sides of the merger or were dominated and controlled by someone who did"; or failed to act in good faith, i.e., where a "'fiduciary intentionally fails to act in the face of a known duty to act, demonstrating a conscious disregard for his duties.'"[59] The Plaintiffs do not allege that any member of the Board--apart from Schaeffer and Newsome--stood on both sides of the transaction. Instead, the Plaintiffs allege that the fourteen disinterested members of the Board who unanimously voted to approve the transaction were dominated and controlled by Schaeffer and acted in bad faith. In particular, the Plaintiffs argue that the Court should infer domination and control by Schaeffer and an intentional dereliction of duty by the Board from the following allegations: the Board approved the change of control severance plan; it accepted the CME's first offer; it permitted Schaeffer and Newsome to "bypass the SIC"; it failed to obtain a "collar" on the stock portion of the merger consideration; and its members were afraid of being terminated because Schaeffer had "forced" a former board member to resign when that member disagreed with Schaeffer regarding a transaction unrelated to the present one.

That directors acquiesce in, or endorse actions by, a chairman of the board--actions that from an outsider's perspective might seem questionable --does not, without more, support an inference of domination by the chairman or the absence of directorial will. The NYMEX directors were otherwise unquestionably independent--this is not an instance where certain relationships raised some concern but not sufficient doubt to sustain a challenge to director independence. In short, the Complaint alleges nothing more than a board which relied upon, and sometimes deferred to, its chairman. It does not allege dominance such that the independence

---

exculpated.").

[59] *See, e.g., Lyondell,* 970 A.2d at 243 (quoting *In re Walt Disney Co. Deriv. Litig.,* 906 A.2d 27, 67 (Del. 2006)).

or good faith of the board may fairly be questioned. The Court concludes that it would be unreasonable to infer from these allegations that the Board was dominated by Schaeffer or that the Board acted in bad faith.

Because the Plaintiffs' allegations are too conclusory to support an inference of domination, the Plaintiffs, at bottom, must seek to convert into a loyalty claim their aversion to the process the Board employed in negotiating the merger. The most that can be inferred from their allegations is that the Board's process was not perfect. However, the Delaware Courts have repeatedly held that "there is no single blueprint that a board must follow to fulfill its duties." In any event, claims of flawed process are properly brought as duty of care, not loyalty, claims and, as discussed, those claims are barred by the exculpatory clause of NYMEX's Certificate of Incorporation. Moreover, to the extent the Complaint alleges that the Board acted in bad faith, such allegations must fail because, based on the facts in the Complaint, it cannot be said that the Board intentionally failed to act in the face of a known duty to act, demonstrating a conscious disregard for its duties. More precisely, the Complaint has not alleged that the Board "utterly failed to obtain the best sale price." Therefore, the Court must grant the Defendants' motion to dismiss the Complaint as to the breaches of fiduciary duty claims.

2.   Claims Against Defendants Schaeffer and Newsome

In addition to the claims brought against them as members of the Board (which are dismissed as failing to state an actionable claim), Defendants Schaeffer and Newsome are alleged to have violated their fiduciary duties through "active participation in wrongdoing" in their joint role as the principal negotiators with CME. Specifically, Plaintiffs allege that Schaeffer and Newsome violated their fiduciary duties by "rejecting and keeping secret CME's secret collar offer, ignoring the SIC, and withholding information regarding strategic opportunities and bids" from fellow directors, as well as in "committing" to CME that NYMEX would not attempt to renegotiate any of the economic terms of the proposed sale and failing to advise the Board of such a commitment, and in entering into an agreement with CME to vote their shares in favor of the proposed acquisition. Schaeffer is additionally alleged to have breached his fiduciary duties by "rejecting NYSE's interest in the Company due to NYSE's failure to abide by his personal demands."

The claim that Schaeffer and Newsome breached their fiduciary duties by being the sole negotiators with CME and not involving the SIC in the consideration or negotiation of the acquisition is dismissed. It is well within the business judgment of the Board to determine how merger negotiations will be conducted, and to delegate the task of negotiating to the Chairman and the Chief Executive Officer. Additionally, as the Court has already found that the Board was clearly independent, there was no requirement to involve an independent committee in negotiations, nor does the existence of such a committee mandate its use. The allegation that Schaeffer and Newsome committed to CME that NYMEX would not renegotiate any of the economic terms of the acquisition is similarly not actionable, since Plaintiffs have not put forth any evidence for how Schaeffer and Newsome were capable of binding NYMEX from seeking to modify the terms of the agreement had the Board wanted to. Finally, as the Complaint does not allege why the act of entering into a voting support agreement is a breach of fiduciary duties, particularly where the economic incentives of directors and shareholders are aligned and where the overall percentage of shares locked-up is not material, this claim is additionally dismissed.

*   *   *

III.   CONCLUSION

For the foregoing reasons, Defendants' motions to dismiss are granted. Implementing orders will be entered.

Add at the end of the Note on page 634:

In Ventas, Inc. v. Health Care Property Investors, Inc., 2007 WL 4547389 (W.D. Ky., 2007) a retirement home owner, Sunrise REIT, put itself up for sale. Each bidder was required to sign a standstill agreement that prohibited it from making any bids outside the auction for 18 months. At the last stages of the process each remaining bidder was required to enter into an agreement with Sunrise Senior Living (SSL), which provided management services for the retirement homes. Only Ventas succeeded in signing such an agreement, and then entered into a purchase agreement with Sunrise for all of its assets at $15 per share. Sunrise informed Health Care Property Investors ("Health Care") of its agreement with Ventas, and that the standstill agreement remained in effect. Nevertheless, Health Care subsequently announced an $18 bid, and Sunrise's shareholders rejected Ventas' bid. Subsequently Ventas increased its offer to $16.50 per share, obtained approval and closed the transaction. It then brought suit against Health Care for tortious interference with contractual relations. Health Care moved to dismiss, and its motion was denied by the district court. The opinion contained the following discussion:

> Defendant's next argument is that Plaintiff has failed to state a claim of tortious interference with contract. Under Kentucky law, in order to make out such a claim Plaintiff must show: (1) the existence of a contract; (2) Defendant's knowledge of this contract; (3) that Defendant intended to cause its breach; (4) that Defendant's conduct caused the breach; (5) that this breach resulted in damages to Plaintiff; and (6) that Defendant had no privilege or justification to excuse its conduct.

> Defendant makes two arguments here. First, Defendant argues that Plaintiff has failed to show that any interference allegedly committed by Defendant was tortious, i.e. without ""privilege or justification."" Second, Defendant argues that Plaintiff has failed to show any breach of the Purchase Agreement by Sunrise REIT.

1.

In making its first argument, Defendant endeavors to portray itself merely as Plaintiff's business competitor, submitting a bid for a company selling itself in the open marketplace. Omitted from this characterization, however, is the critical and apparently undisputed fact that Defendant was bound by its Standstill Agreement with Sunrise REIT at the time Defendant submitted and publicized its bid. The Court agrees with Defendant that no special tort duty was owed to Plaintiff by Defendant due merely to the existence of Defendant's Standstill Agreement with Sunrise REIT, but finds that the allegation that Defendant broke the "rules of the game" to which Defendant had agreed is nevertheless sufficiently consistent with the "no privilege or justification" element of Plaintiff's claim as to preclude dismissal."

Insert in Chapter 8, Part 2.C., at page 661, at the end of Note:

During the growth of Management Buyouts financed by private equity firms some sellers have been insisting on (and getting) "go-shop" provisions that permit the seller to actively shop the company after signing a definitive agreement. Commentators suggest that this phenomenon has developed because a strong sellers' market has existed in the period 2005-07, with the availability of cheap financing because of low interest rates, the huge growth in private equity funds seeking acquisitions accompanied by growth in "strategic acquisitions" by other operating companies, as opposed to "financial acquisitions" by private equity funds. Stephen J. Glover & Jonathan P. Goodman, Go-Shops: Are They Here to Stay?, 11 No. 6 The M&A Lawyer 1 (June 2007).

The authors describe the go-shop periods as being from 20 to 50 days, and suggest that the length of the shopping period should probably depend on how extensively the company was shopped before entering into a definitive agreement. In some cases the go-shop period is followed by a fiduciary out period, during which the company can consider unsolicited bids, which would include bids from those contacted during the go-shop period. These agreements are sometimes accompanied by a reduced termination fee if the target accepts a superior bid during the go-shop period, in the range of 40% to 60% of the full termination fee payable after that time. Maytag Corporation entered into such an agreement with Ripplewood Capital. Some of the important provisions are quoted below:

"SECTION 5.02. NO SOLICITATION. (a) During the period beginning on the date of this Agreement and continuing until 12:01 a.m. (EST) on June 18, 2005 (the "SOLICITATION PERIOD END DATE"), the Company and any officer, director or employee of, or any investment banker, attorney or other advisor or representative (collectively, "REPRESENTATIVES") of, the Company or any Company Subsidiary shall be permitted to (i) directly or indirectly solicit, initiate or encourage the submission of a Company Takeover Proposal and (ii) directly or indirectly participate in discussions or negotiations regarding, and furnish to any person information with respect to, and take any other action to facilitate any inquiries or the making of any proposal that constitutes, or may reasonably be expected to lead to, a Company Takeover Proposal; PROVIDED, HOWEVER, that (A) the Company shall not, nor shall it authorize or permit any Company Subsidiary to, nor shall it authorize or permit any Representative of the Company or any Company Subsidiary to, provide to any person any non-public information (other than any immaterial non-public information) with respect to the Company or any Company Subsidiary without first entering into a customary confidentiality agreement with such person that is not less restrictive of the other party than the Confidentiality Agreement (excluding the provisions of the eleventh paragraph thereof) and (B) the Company shall promptly provide to Parent any non-public information concerning the Company or any Company Subsidiary that is provided to such person or its Representatives which was not previously provided to Parent.

"(b) Subject to Section 5.02(c), from the Solicitation Period End Date until the earlier of the Effective Time and the termination of this Agreement pursuant to Article VIII, the Company shall not, nor shall it authorize or permit any Company Subsidiary to, and the Company shall direct and use its reasonable best efforts to cause the Representatives of the Company or any Company Subsidiary not to, (i) directly or indirectly solicit, initiate or encourage the submission of any Company Takeover Proposal, (ii) enter into any agreement with respect to any Company Takeover Proposal or (iii) directly or indirectly participate in any discussions or negotiations regarding, or furnish to any person any non-public information with respect to, or knowingly take any other action to facilitate any inquiries or the making of any proposal that constitutes, or may reasonably be expected to lead to, any Company Takeover Proposal. Without limiting the foregoing, it is agreed that any violation of the restrictions set forth in the preceding sentence by any Representative of the Company or any Company Subsidiary, whether or not such person is purporting to act on behalf of the Company or any Company Subsidiary or otherwise, shall be deemed to be a breach of this Section 5.02(b) by the Company. Subject to Section 5.02(c), on the Solicitation Period End Date, the Company shall immediately cease and cause to be terminated any existing solicitation, encouragement, discussion, negotiation or other action permitted by Section 5.02(a) conducted by the Company, any Company Subsidiary or any of their respective Representatives with respect to a

Company Takeover Proposal.

"(c) Notwithstanding anything to the contrary in Section 5.02(b), from the Solicitation Period End Date and prior to the receipt of the Company Stockholder Approval, the Company may, in response to an unsolicited Company Takeover Proposal which did not result from a breach of Section 5.02(b), or a solicited Company Takeover Proposal which did not result from a breach of Section 5.02(a), and which, in either case, the Company Board determines, in good faith, after consultation with outside counsel and financial advisors, may reasonably be expected to lead to a transaction (i) more favorable from a financial point of view to the holders of Company Common Stock than the Merger, taking into account all the terms and conditions of such proposal, and this Agreement (including any amendment to the terms of this Agreement and the Merger in effect as of the date of such determination) and (ii) that is reasonably capable of being completed, taking into account all financial, regulatory, legal and other aspects of such proposal, and subject to compliance with Section 5.02(e), (x) furnish information with respect to the Company and the Company Subsidiaries to the person making such Company Takeover Proposal and its Representatives pursuant to a customary confidentiality agreement not less restrictive of the other party than the Confidentiality Agreement (excluding the provisions of the eleventh paragraph thereof) and (y) participate in discussions or negotiations with such person and its Representatives regarding any Company Takeover Proposal; PROVIDED, HOWEVER, that the Company shall promptly provide to Parent any non-public information concerning the Company or any Company Subsidiary that is provided to the person making such Company Takeover Proposal or its Representatives which was not previously provided to Parent.

"(d) Subject to Section 8.01(e), neither the Company Board nor any committee thereof shall (i) withdraw or modify in a manner adverse to Parent or Sub, or publicly propose to withdraw or modify in a manner adverse to Parent or Sub, the approval or recommendation by the Company Board or any such committee of this Agreement or the Merger, (ii) approve any letter of intent, agreement in principle, acquisition agreement or similar agreement relating to any Company Takeover Proposal or (iii) approve or recommend, or publicly propose to approve or recommend, any Company Takeover Proposal. Notwithstanding the foregoing, if, prior to receipt of the Company Stockholder Approval, the Company Board determines in good faith, after consultation with outside counsel, that failure to so withdraw or modify its recommendation of the Merger and this Agreement would be inconsistent with the Company Board's exercise of its fiduciary duties, the Company Board or any committee thereof may withdraw or modify its recommendation of the Merger and this Agreement.

"(e) The Company promptly shall advise Parent orally and in writing of any Company Takeover Proposal or, following the Solicitation Period End Date, any inquiry with respect to or that would reasonably be expected to lead to any Company Takeover Proposal, the identity of the person making any such Company Takeover Proposal or inquiry and the material terms of any such Company Takeover Proposal or inquiry. The Company shall keep Parent reasonably informed of the status (including any change to the terms thereof) of any such Company Takeover Proposal or inquiry.

"(f) Nothing contained in this Section 5.02 shall prohibit the Company from taking and disclosing to its stockholders a position contemplated by Rule 14e-2(a) promulgated under the Exchange Act or from making any required disclosure to the Company's stockholders if, in the good faith judgment of the Company Board, after consultation with outside counsel, failure so to disclose would be inconsistent with its obligations under applicable Law."

IN RE: LEAR CORPORATION SHAREHOLDER LITIGATION

926 A.2d 94 Del. Ch. 2007)

STRINE, Vice Chancellor.

I.   Introduction

[Lear Corporation is one of the leading automotive parts suppliers in the world, although its business is concentrated with U.S. manufacturers, and to a large extent consists of supplying parts for light trucks and SUVs. As sales of these vehicles have declined with the rise in gas prices, so have Lear's sales suffered. At the same time, large amounts of Lear's debt were maturing. There were rumors of possible bankruptcy. By 2005 Lear was engaged in a restructuring to keep itself solvent. In 2005 Lear's board hired J. P. Morgan Securities, Inc. ("JP Morgan" to provide advisory services on a restructuring, which included divesting underperforming business units and restructuring of its debt, which continued into 2006.]

In early 2006, [Carl] Icahn took a large, public position in Lear stock, with initial purchases at $16-17 per share. Given Icahn's history of prodding issuers toward value-maximizing measures, this news bolstered Lear's flagging stock price, causing it to rise to $21 per share in July, 2006.. Later in 2006, Icahn deepened his investment in Lear, by purchasing $200 million of its stock -- raising his holdings to 24% -- through a secondary offering in which the company sold him stock at $23,

The funds raised in that private placement were used by Lear to reduce its debt and help with its ongoing restructuring.

Icahn's purchase led the stock market to believe that a sale of the company had become likely, leading the stock to trade higher, reaching $30 within a few days of his purchase, and trading in that range during the remainder of 2006. Icahn's investment also combined with another reality: Lear's board had eliminated the corporation's poison pill in 2004, and promised not to reinstate it except in very limited circumstances.

In early 2007, Icahn suggested to Lear's CEO [Rossiter] that a going private transaction might be in Lear's best interest. After a week of discussions, Lear's CEO told the rest of the board. The board formed a Special Committee, which authorized the CEO to negotiate merger terms with Icahn.

During those negotiations, Icahn only moved modestly from his initial offering price of $35 per share, going to $36 per share after Rossiter rejected his initial offer and went to the Special Committee for instructions. Several directors thought the price should be between $36 and $38. When Rossiter informed Icahn that the Special Committee had rejected his bid, Icahn countered at $35.25. Rossiter rejected that bid immediately based on the Special Committee's suggested range, and later in the same telephone call Icahn offered $36, which he said was his highest and best price. Rossiter took that bid to the Special Committee, With advice from JP Morgan, the Special Committee took into account the gloomy projections for both the industry and Lear, and recommended the bid to the full board. Icahn indicated that if the board desired to conduct a pre-signing auction, it was free to do that, but he would pull his offer. But Icahn made it clear that he would allow the company to freely shop his bid after signing, during a so-called go-shop period, but only so long as he received a termination fee of approximately 3%. In view of the fact that Icahn's bid was twice the stock's price before he began to purchase Lear stock, the board feared that if they rejected his bid and started an auction, the stock would fall back down, and he would come in later at a lower price. Over the next few days while detailed merger negotiations took place, the board authorized JP Morgan to engage in a quick search for other buyers. No serious expressions of interest appeared. At the end of the process JP Morgan gave its opinion that $36 was fair, and the board approved the transaction, with its "go shop" and "window shop" provisions, and a termination fee.]

The board did the deal on those terms. After signing, the board's financial advisors aggressively shopped Lear to both financial and strategic buyers. None made a topping bid during the go shop period. Since that time, Lear has been free to entertain an unsolicited superior bid. None has been made.

Stockholders plaintiffs have moved to enjoin the upcoming merger vote, arguing that the Lear board breached its *Revlon* duties and has failed to disclose material facts necessary for the stockholders to cast an informed vote.

In this decision, I largely reject the plaintiffs' claims. Although the Lear Special Committee made an infelicitous decision to permit the CEO to negotiate the merger terms outside the presence of Special Committee supervision, there is no evidence that that decision adversely affected the overall reasonableness of the board's efforts to secure the highest possible value. The board retained for itself broad leeway to shop the company after signing, and negotiated deal protection measures that did not present an unreasonable barrier to any second-arriving bidder. Moreover, the board obtained Icahn's agreement to vote his equity position for any bid superior to his own that was embraced by the board, thus signaling Icahn's own willingness to be a seller at the right price. Given the circumstances faced by Lear, the decision of the board to lock in the potential for its stockholders to receive $36 per share with the right for the board to hunt for more emerges as reasonable. The board's post-signing market check was a reasonable one that provided adequate assurance that no bidder willing to materially top Icahn existed. Thus, I conclude that it is unlikely that the plaintiffs would, after trial, succeed on their claims relating to the sale process.

* * *

II. Factual Background

* * *

C. The Merger Terms

1. The Merger Agreement

The Merger Agreement grants Icahn two primary deal protections for allowing its offer to be used as a stalking horse: a termination fee payable if Lear accepted a superior proposal from another bidder and matching rights in the event that a superior proposal is presented. In exchange, the Lear board secured an ability to actively solicit interest from third parties for 45 days (the so-called "go-shop" period), a fiduciary out that permitted the board to accept an unsolicited superior third-party bid after the go-shop period ended, a reverse termination fee payable if AREP [American Real Estate Partners, LP, Icahn's acquisition vehicle] breached the Merger Agreement, and a voting agreement that required Icahn, AREP, and their affiliates to vote their shares in favor of any superior proposal that AREP did not match.

The termination fee that AREP would be entitled to depended on the nature and timing of Lear's termination of the Merger Agreement. Both parties had a right to terminate the Merger Agreement if that Agreement was not approved by Lear's stockholders, but if no superior transaction was completed within a year of the negative stockholder vote, no termination fee was due. If, however, a superior proposal was accepted by Lear such that the company "substantially concurrently" terminated the Merger Agreement and entered into an alternate acquisition agreement, AREP was entitled to a termination fee contingent on the timing of termination. Likewise, AREP could claim a break-up fee if the Lear board withdrew its support (or failed to reconfirm its support when requested to do so) for the AREP offer.

In the event that AREP was entitled to a termination fee, the amount of that fee depended on the timing of the termination of the Merger Agreement. If the Agreement was terminated during the go-shop period, Lear was required to pay to AREP a fee of $73.5 million plus up to $6 million in reasonable and documented expenses. At most, this amounted to a payment of $79.5 million, which is 2.79% of the equity value of the transaction or 1.9% of the total $4.1 billion enterprise value of the deal. In the alternative, if the merger was called off after the go-shop period ended, AREP was entitled to a higher fee of $85,225 million as well as up to $15 million in expense reimbursements. This payment of roughly $100 million amounted to 3.52% of the equity, or 2.4% of the enterprise, valuation of Lear. Viewed in light of the 79.8 million Lear shares outstanding on a fully diluted basis at the time of the merger, the $79.5 million break-up fee due upon termination during the go-shop period translated into a willingness to pay a little less than a dollar more than Icahn's $36 bid. The $100 million fee equated to a bid increase of roughly $1.25 per share.

In addition to these termination fees, AREP was protected by a contractual right to match certain superior bids that Lear received. If Lear fielded a superior proposal, the Merger Agreement forced Lear to notify AREP of the proposal's terms and afforded AREP ten days to determine whether it would increase its offer to match the superior terms. If the superior proposal was in excess of $37 per share, AREP only had a single chance to match, but if it did not cross that threshold, Lear was obligated to allow AREP three days to match each successive bid. In the event that AREP decided not a match a superior proposal, it was obligated to vote its bloc of shares in favor of that transaction under the voting agreement it executed in combination with the Merger Agreement. The combination of match rights with the voting agreement signaled the willingness of Icahn to be either a buyer or seller in a transaction involving Lear.

In exchange for the protections that Icahn and AREP received, the Merger Agreement permitted the Lear board to pursue other buyers for 45 days and then to passively consider unsolicited bids until the merger closed. But, once that 45-day window closed, a second phase, which might be called a "no-shop" or "window-shop" period, began during which the Lear board retained the right to accept an unsolicited superior proposal.

Lear was also protected in the event that AREP breached the Merger Agreement's terms by a reverse termination fee of $250 million. That fee would be triggered if AREP failed to satisfy the closing conditions in the Merger Agreement, was unable to secure financing for the $4.1 billion transaction, or otherwise breached the Agreement. But AREP's liability to Lear was limited to its right to receive this fee.

* * *

III. Legal Analysis

* * *

B. The Plaintiffs' Revlon Claims

* * *

Although I do not, as will soon be seen, view this negotiation process as a disaster warranting the issuance of an injunction, it is far from ideal and unnecessarily raises concerns about the integrity and skill of those trying to represent Lear's public investors. In reflecting on why this approach was taken, I consider it less than coincidental that Rossiter did not tell the board about Icahn's interest in making a going private proposal until seven days after it was expressed. Although a week seems a short period of time, it is not in this deal context. In seven days, a newly formed Special Committee's advisors can help the Committee do a lot of thinking about how to go about things and what the Committee should seek to achieve; that includes thinking about the Committee's price and deal term objectives, and the most effective way to reach them.

The Lear Special Committee was deprived of important deliberative and tactical time, and, as a result, it quickly decided on an approach to the process not dissimilar to those taken on most issues that come before corporate boards that do not involve conflicts of interest. That is, the directors allowed the actual work to be done by management and signed off on it after the fact. But the work that Rossiter was doing was not like most work. It involved the sale of the company in circumstances in which Rossiter (and his top subordinates) had economic interests that were not shared by Lear's public stockholders.[*]

Acknowledging all that, though, I am not persuaded that the Special Committee's less-than-ideal approach to the price negotiations with Icahn makes it likely that the plaintiffs, after a trial, will be able to demonstrate a *Revlon* breach. To fairly determine whether the defendants breached their *Revlon* obligations, I must consider the entirety of their actions in attempting to secure the highest price reasonably available to the corporation. Reasonableness, not perfection, measured in business terms relevant to value creation, rather than by what creates the most

---

[*]   Shortly before Icahn expressed an interest in an acquisition, Rossiter asked the board to change his employment arrangements to allow him to cash in his retirement benefits, which were unfunded and had a nominal value of $10 million if he retired at that time. But if Lear filed for bankruptcy, he became an unsecured creditor, with little chance of receiving the benefits. Rossiter also had severance payments of $15.1 million in the event of a change of control. - Ed.

sterile smell, is the metric.[19]

When that metric is applied, I find that the plaintiffs have not demonstrated a reasonable probability of success on their *Revlon* claim. The overall approach to obtaining the best price taken by the Special Committee appears, for reasons I now explain, to have been reasonable.

First, as many institutional investors and corporate law professors have advocated that all public corporations should do, Lear had gotten rid of its poison pill in 2004. Although it is true that the Lear board had reserved the right to reinstate a pill upon a vote of the stockholders or of a majority of the board's independent directors, it was hardly in a position to do that lightly, given the potential for such action to upset institutional investors and the influential proxy advisory firm, ISS.[20] At the very least, Lear's public elimination of its pill signaled a willingness to ponder the merits of unsolicited offers. That factor is one that the Lear board was entitled to take into account in designing its approach to value maximization.

Relatedly, Icahn's investment moves in 2006 also stirred the pot, as the plaintiffs admit. Indeed, they go so far as to acknowledge that Lear could be perceived as having been on sale from April 2006 onward. As the plaintiffs also admit, Icahn has over the years displayed a willingness to buy when that is to his advantage and to sell when that is to his advantage. The M&A markets know this. Icahn's entry as a player in the Lear drama would have drawn attention from buyers with a potential interest in investing in the automobile sector.

In considering whether to sign up a deal with Icahn at $36 or insist on a full pre-signing auction, these factors were relevant. No one had asked Lear to the dance other than Icahn as of that point, even though it was perfectly obvious that Lear was open to invitations. Although a formal auction was the clearest way to signal a desire for bids, it also presented the risk of losing Icahn's $36 bid. If Icahn was going to be put into an auction, he could reasonably argue that he would pull his bid and see what others thought of Lear before making his move. If the response to the auction was underwhelming, he might then pick up the company at a lower price.

The Lear board's concern about this possibility was, in my view, reasonable, given the lack of, with one exception, even a soft overture from a potential buyer

---

[19]   *E.g., QVC,* 637 A.2d at 45 ("[C]ourt[s] applying enhanced judicial scrutiny should be deciding whether the directors made a reasonable decision, not a perfect decision. If a board selected one of several reasonable alternatives, a court should not second-guess that choice even though it might have decided otherwise or subsequent events may have cast doubt on the board's determination.").

[20]   ISS is "Institutional Shareholder Services," which provides voting advice to institutional investors, and promulgates an extensive set of corporate governance standards. - Ed.

other than Icahn in 2006. That exception was a call that Rossiter had gotten from Cerberus when Lear's market price was still well below $20 per share. But that exception is interesting in itself. Once Icahn's second investment became public and his deepened position was announced in October 2006, Cerberus never made a move. Likewise, when Cerberus was contacted during the pre-signing market check and as part of the go-shop process, it never signaled a hunger for Lear or a price at which it would be willing to do a deal.

Also relevant to the question of whether an auction was advisable was the lack of ardor that other major Lear stockholders had for the opportunity to buy equity in the secondary offering along with Icahn. That Lear is worth $60 per share, an idea whose implications I will discuss, they passed on the chance to buy additional stock at $23 per share in October 2006. Given this history, I cannot conclude that it was unreasonable for the Lear board not to demand a full auction before signing its Merger Agreement with Icahn. There were important risks counseling against such an insistence, especially if the board could to some extent have it both ways by locking in a floor of $36 per share while securing a chance to prospect for more.

Second, I likewise find that the plaintiffs have not demonstrated a likelihood of success on their argument that the Lear board acted unreasonably in agreeing to the deal protections in the Merger Agreement rather than holding out for even greater flexibility to look for a higher bid after signing with Icahn. In so finding, I give relatively little weight to the two-tiered nature of the termination fee. The go-shop period was truncated and left a bidder hard-pressed to do adequate due diligence, present a topping bid with a full-blown draft merger agreement, have the Lear board make the required decision to declare the new bid a superior offer, wait Icahn's ten-day period to match, and then have the Lear board accept that bid, terminate its agreement with Icahn, and "substantially concurrently" enter into a merger agreement with it. All of these events had to occur within the go-shop period for the bidder to benefit from the lower termination fee. This was not a provision that gave a lower break fee to a bidder who entered the process in some genuine way during the go-shop period -- for example, by signing up a confidentiality stipulation and completing some of the key steps toward the achievement of a definitive merger agreement at a superior price. Rather, it was a provision that essentially required the bidder to get the whole shebang done within the 45-day window. It is conceivable, I suppose, that this could occur if a ravenous bidder had simply been waiting for an explicit invitation to swallow up Lear. But if that sort of Kobayashi-like buyer existed, it might have reasonably been expected to emerge before the Merger Agreement with Icahn was signed based on Lear's lack of a rights plan and the publicity given to Icahn's prior investments in the company.

That said, I do not find convincing the plaintiffs' argument that the combination of the fuller termination fee that would be payable for a bid meeting the required conditions after the go-shop period with Icahn's contractual match right were bid-chilling. The termination fee in that scenario amounts to 3.5% of equity value and 2.4% of enterprise value. For purposes of considering the preclusive effect of a termination fee on a rival bidder, it is arguably more important to look at the enterprise value metric because, as is the case with Lear, most acquisitions require the buyer to pay for the company's equity and refinance all of its debt. But regardless of whether that is the case, the percentage of either measure the termination fee represents here is hardly of the magnitude that should deter a serious rival bid. The plaintiffs' claim to the contrary is based on the median of termination fees identified in a presentation made by JPMorgan in two-tiered post-signing processes of 1.8% of equity value during the go-shop period and 2.9% thereafter. The plaintiffs also state that Icahn should have gotten a lower fee because he would profit from a topping bid through his equity stake. These factors are not ones that I believe would, after trial, convince me that the board's decision to accede to Icahn's demand for a 3.5% fee (2.8% during the go-shop) was unreasonable. Icahn was tying up $1.4 billion in capital to make a bid for a corporation in a troubled industry, was agreeing to allow the target to shop the company freely for 45 days and to continue to work freely with Lear concerning any emerging bidders during that process, and was agreeing to vote his shares for any superior bid accepted by the Lear board.

Likewise, match rights are hardly novel and have been upheld by this court when coupled with termination fees despite the additional obstacle they are present.[20] And, in this case, the match right was actually a limited one that encouraged bidders to top Icahn in a material way. As described, a bidder whose initial topping move was over $37 could limit Icahn to only one chance to match. Therefore, a bidder who was truly willing to make a materially greater bid than Icahn had it within its means to short-circuit the match right process. Given all those factors, and the undisputed reality that second bidders have been able to succeed in the face of a termination fee/matching right combination of this potency,[21] I am skeptical that a trial record would convince me that the Lear board acted unreasonably in assenting to the termination fee and match right provisions in the Merger Agreement.

*   *   *

Finally, the plaintiffs have attempted to persuade me that the Lear board has likely breached its *Revlon* duties because the it had hoped that Icahn would offer

---

[20]   *E.g., In re Toys 'R' Us, Inc. S'holder Litig.,* 877 A.2d 975, 980 (Del. Ch. 2005) (finding that inclusion of a termination fee and the presence of matching rights in a merger agreement did not act as a serious barrier to any bidder willing to pay materially more for the target entity).

[21]   Defendants have cited 15 transactions within the past three years in which intervening bids were made despite termination fees of 3% or more and contractual match rights in the merger agreements.

more than $36 per share, that some Lear stockholders think that $36 per share is too low, and because the plaintiffs have presented a valuation expert opining that the value of Lear was in the high-$30s to mid-$40s range. This is not an appraisal proceeding, and I have no intention to issue my own opinion as to Lear's value.

But what I have done is reviewed the record on valuation carefully. Lear is one of the nation's largest corporations. Before Icahn emerged, the stock market had abundant information about Lear and its future prospects. It valued Lear at much less than $36 per share -- around $17 per share in March and April 2006. After Icahn emerged, the stock market perceived that Lear had greater value based on Icahn's interest and the likelihood of a change of control transaction involving a purchase of all of the firm's equity, not just daily trades in minority shares.

Although the $36 price may have been below what the Lear board hoped to achieve, they had a reasonable basis to accept it. The valuation information in the record, when fairly read, does not incline me toward a finding that the Lear board was unreasonable in accepting the Icahn bid. Although the plaintiffs' valuation expert originally opined that a fair range would be in the "high-$30s" to "mid-$40s," his DCF analysis suggests a range below the merger price, once that DCF analysis is properly adjusted to correct for errors in computing the discount rate he himself admits were either in error or inconsistent. When corrected to use an appropriate discount rate and to consider current industry circumstances, the plaintiff's own expert's DCF value for Lear based on its Long Range Plan with Current Industry Outlook ranges from $27.13 to $35.75. Moreover, to the extent that plaintiffs' expert relies upon the $45.19 median of his DCF models, that reliance appears questionable as those models produce a range between $9.81 and $107.54 per share.

At this stage, the more important point is this. The Lear board had sufficient evidence to conclude that it was better to accept $36 if a topping bid did not emerge than to risk having Lear's stock price return to the level that existed before the market drew the conclusion that Lear would be sold because Icahn had bought such a substantial stake. Putting aside the market check, the $36 per share price appears as a reasonable one on this record, when traditional measures of valuation, such as the DCF, are considered. More important, however, is that the $36 price has been and is still being subjected to a real world market check, which is unimpeded by bid-deterring factors.

If, as the plaintiffs say, their expert is correct that Lear is worth materially more than $36 per share and that some major stockholders believe that Lear is worth $60 per share, a major chance to make huge profits is being missed by those stockholders and by the market for corporate control in general. While it may be that that is the case, I cannot premise an injunction on the Lear board's refusal to act on an improbability of that kind. Stockholders who have a different view on value may freely communicate with others, subject to their compliance with the securities laws, about their different views on value. Stockholders may vote no and seek appraisal. But the plaintiffs are in no position ask me to refuse the Lear electorate the chance to freely determine whether a guaranteed $36 per share right now is preferable to the risks of continued ownership of Lear stock.

VI.   Conclusion

For the foregoing reasons, the plaintiffs' motion for a preliminary injunction is largely denied, with the exception that a preliminary injunction will issue preventing the merger vote until supplemental disclosure of the kind required by the decision is issued.[*] The defendants shall provide the court on June 18 their proposal as to the form of that disclosure, and the timing of its provision to stockholders. So long as the court is satisfied about substance and timing, the merger vote may be able to proceed as currently scheduled. The plaintiffs and defendants shall collaborate on an implementing order, which shall be presented on June 18 as well.

QUESTIONS

1.   Note there are three stages to termination fees: (1) a period during which Lear can terminated without payment of a termination fee; (2) a period when the fee of 2.79% of the cost of Lear's equity; and (3) a fee of approximately $3.52% of Lear's equity. What was the purpose of the three-tier fee arrangement?

2.   What were the conditions that would obligate Icahn to pay a reverse termination fee of $250 million, or approximately 6% of the $4.1 million purchase price?

3.   Why would Lear enter into a reverse termination fee of $250 million when its losses, assuming the stock would return to its pre-Icahn price, would be approximately half of the $4.1 billion purchase price?

Add on page 845, after Questions following Weinberger v. UOP, Inc.:

Gantler v. Stephens

965 A.2d 695 (Del. 2009)

Before STEELE, Chief Justice, HOLLAND, BERGER, JACOBS and RIDGELY, Justices, constituting the Court en Banc.

---

[*]   Additional disclosures about Rossiter's retirement and severance arrangements were required. - Ed.

JACOBS, Justice:

The plaintiffs in this breach of fiduciary duty action, who are certain shareholders of First Niles Financial, Inc. ("First Niles" or the "Company"), appeal from the dismissal of their complaint by the Court of Chancery The complaint alleges that the defendants, who are officers and directors of First Niles, violated their fiduciary duties by rejecting a valuable opportunity to sell the Company, *Issue* deciding instead to reclassify the Company's shares in order to benefit themselves, and by disseminating a materially misleading proxy statement to induce shareholder approval. We conclude that the complaint pleads sufficient facts to overcome the *—Holding* business judgment presumption, and to state substantive fiduciary duty and disclosure claims. We therefore reverse the Court of Chancery's judgment of dismissal and remand the case for further proceedings consistent with this Opinion.

Factual and Procedural Background

A. The Parties

First Niles, a Delaware corporation headquartered in Niles, Ohio, is a holding company whose sole business is to own and operate the Home Federal Savings and Loan Association of Niles ("Home Federal" or the "Bank"). The Bank is a federally chartered stock savings association that operates a single branch in Niles, Ohio.

The plaintiffs (Leonard T. Gander and his wife, Patricia A. Cetrone; John and Patricia Gernat; and Paul and Marsha Mitchell) collectively own 121,715 First Niles shares. Plaintiff Gander was a First Niles director from April 2003 until April 2006.

Defendant William L. Stephens is the Chairman of the Board, President and CEO of both First Niles and the Bank, and has been employed by the Bank since 1969. Defendant P. James Kramer, a director of First Niles and the Bank since 1994, is president of William Kramer & Son, a heating and air conditioning company in Niles that provides heating and air conditioning services to the Bank. Defendant William S. Eddy has been a director of First Niles and the Bank since 2002. Defendant Daniel E. Csontos has been a director of First Niles and the Bank since April 2006. Csontos has also been a full-time employee, serving as compliance officer and corporate secretary of both institutions since 1996 and 2003, respectively. Defendant Robert I. Shaker, who became a director of First Niles and the Bank in January of 2006 after former director Ralph A. Zuzolo passed away, is a principal of a law firm in Niles, Ohio. Defendant Lawrence Safarek is the Treasurer and Vice President of both First Niles and the Bank.

Until his death in August of 2005, Mr. Zuzolo (who is not a party) was a director and corporate board secretary of First Niles and the Bank. Zuzolo was also both a principal in the law firm of Zuzolo, Zuzolo & Zuzolo, and the CEO and sole owner of American Title Services, Inc., a real estate title company in Niles, Ohio. Zuzolo's law firm frequently provided legal services to the Bank, and American

Title provided title services for nearly all of the Bank's real estate closings.

B. Exploring a Potential Sale of First Niles

In late 2003, First Niles was operating in a depressed local economy, with little to no growth in the Bank's assets and anticipated low growth for the future. At that time Stephens, who was Chairman, President, CEO and founder of First Niles and the Bank, was beyond retirement age and there was no heir apparent among the Company's officers. The acquisition market for banks like Home Federal was brisk, however, and First Niles was thought to be an excellent acquisition for another financial institution. Accordingly, the First Niles Board sought advice on strategic opportunities available to the Company, and in August 2004, decided that First Niles should put itself up for sale (the "Sales Process").

After authorizing the sale of the Company, the First Niles Board specially retained an investment bank, Keefe, Bruyette & Woods (the "Financial Advisor"), and a law firm, Silver, Freedman & Taft ("Legal Counsel"). At the next Board meeting in September 2004, Management advocated abandoning the Sales Process in favor of a proposal to "privatize" the Company. Under Management's proposal, First Niles would delist its shares from the NASDAQ SmallCap Market, convert the Bank from a federally chartered to a state chartered bank, and reincorporate in Maryland. The Board did not act on that proposal, and the Sales Process continued.

[The details of an abortive search, where three potential buyers were located, but none of the leads were ultimately pursued are set in in the Note on this case, supra at page 22 of this Supplement. While the board "investigated" the prospects of a sale in a manner that was allegedly lethargic, at best, management failed to cooperate in due diligence sought by the prospective buyers, and instead sought a "going private" transaction through a recapitalization in which all small shareholders would receive non-voting preferred stock. We resume this account where the board determined to reject the best outstanding offer, and pursue a going private transaction. We also omit the court's ruling that Count I, which addressed the abandonment of these sale efforts, stated a valid claim for relief.]

*   *   *

C. The Reclassification Proposal

Five weeks later, on April 18, 2005, Stephens circulated to the Board members a document describing a proposed privatization of First Niles ("Privatization Proposal"). That Proposal recommended reclassifying the shares of holders of 300 or fewer shares of First Niles common stock into a new issue of Series A Preferred Stock on a one-to-one basis (the "Reclassification"). The Series A Preferred Stock would pay higher dividends and have the same liquidation rights as the common stock, but the Preferred holders would lose all voting rights except in the event of a proposed sale of the Company. The Privatization Proposal claimed that the Reclassification was the best method to privatize the Company because it allowed maximum flexibility for future capital management activities, such as open market purchases and negotiated buy-backs. Moreover, First Niles could achieve the Reclassification without having to buy back shares in a fair market appraisal.

On April 20, 2005, the Board appointed Zuzolo to chair a special committee to investigate issues relating to the Reclassification, specifically: (1) reincorporating in a state other than Delaware, (2) changing the Bank's charter from a federal to a state charter, (3) deregistering from NASDAQ, and (4) delisting. However, Zuzolo passed away before any other directors were appointed to the special committee.

On December 5, 2005, Powell Goldstein, First Niles' outside counsel specially retained for the Privatization ("Outside Counsel"), orally presented the Reclassification proposal to the Board. The Board was not furnished any written materials. After the presentation, the Board voted 3 to 1 to direct Outside Counsel to proceed with the Reclassification program. Gantler cast the only dissenting vote.

Thereafter, the makeup of the Board changed. Shaker replaced Zuzolo in January of 2006, and Csontos replaced Gantler in April of 2006. From that point on, the Board consisted of Stephens, Kramer, Eddy, Shaker and Csontos.

On June 5, 2006, the Board determined, based on the advice of Management and First Niles' general counsel, that the Reclassification was fair both to the First Niles shareholders who would receive newly issued Series A Preferred Stock, and to those shareholders who would continue to hold First Niles common stock. On June 19, the Board voted unanimously to amend the Company's certificate of incorporation to reclassify the shares held by owners of 300 or fewer shares of common stock into shares of Series A Preferred Stock that would have the features and terms described in the Privatization Proposal.

D. The Reclassification Proxy and the Shareholder Vote

On June 29, 2006, the Board submitted a preliminary proxy to the United States Securities and Exchange Commission ("SEC"). An amended version of the preliminary proxy was filed on August 10. Plaintiffs initiated this lawsuit after the amended filing, claiming that the preliminary proxy was materially false and misleading in various respects. On November 16, 2006, the Board, after correcting some of the alleged deficiencies, disseminated a definitive proxy statement ("Reclassification Proxy" or "Proxy") to the First Niles shareholders. On November 20, the plaintiffs filed an amended complaint, alleging (inter alia) that the Reclassification Proxy contained material misstatements and omissions.

In the Reclassification Proxy, the Board represented that the proposed Reclassification would allow First Niles to "save significant legal, accounting and administrative expenses" relating to public disclosure and reporting requirements under the Exchange Act. The Proxy also disclosed the benefits of deregistration as including annual savings of $ 142,500 by reducing the number of common shareholders, $ 81,000 by avoiding Sarbanes-Oxley related compliance costs, and $ 174,000 by avoiding a one-time consulting fee to design a system to improve the Company's internal control structure. The negative features and estimated costs of the transaction included $ 75,000 in Reclassification-related expenses, reduced liquidity for both the to-be-reclassified preferred and common shares, and the loss of certain investor protections under the federal securities laws.

The Reclassification Proxy also disclosed alternative transactions that the Board had considered, including a cash-out merger, a reverse stock-split, an issue tender offer, expense reduction and a business combination. The Proxy stated that each of the directors and officers of First Niles had "a conflict of interest with respect to [the Reclassification] because he or she is in a position to structure it in such a way that benefits his or her interests differently from the interests of unaffiliated shareholders." The Proxy further disclosed that the Company had received one firm merger offer, and that "[a]fter careful deliberations, the board determined in its business judgment the proposal was not in the best interests of the Company or our shareholders and rejected the proposal."

The Company's shareholders approved the Reclassification on December 14, 2006. Taking judicial notice of the Company's Rule 13e-3 Transaction Statement,[5] the trial court concluded that of the 1,384,533 shares outstanding and eligible to vote, 793,092 shares (or 57.3%) were voted in favor and 11,060 shares abstained. Of the unaffiliated shares, however, the proposal passed by a bare 50.28% majority vote.

E. Procedural History

The amended complaint asserts three separate claims. Count I alleges that the defendants breached their fiduciary duties to the First Niles shareholders by rejecting the First Place merger offer and abandoning the Sales Process. Count II alleges that the defendants breached their fiduciary duty of disclosure by disseminating a materially false and misleading Reclassification Proxy. Count III alleges that the defendants breached their fiduciary duties by effecting the Reclassification.

The defendants moved to dismiss the complaint in its entirety. Defendants argued that Counts I and III were legally deficient for failure to allege facts sufficient to overcome the business judgment presumption; that Count II failed to state a claim that the Reclassification Proxy was materially false and misleading; and that Count III should also be dismissed because the First Niles shareholders had "ratified" the Board's decision to reclassify the First Niles shares. The Court of Chancery credited these arguments and dismissed the complaint. This appeal followed.

ANALYSIS

---

[5] Rules promulgated under the Exchange Act require the filing of a Rule 13e-3 transaction statement for any transaction that may result in a company reclassifying any of its securities. *See* 17 C.F.R. § 240.13e-3 (2008) ("Going Private Transactions by Certain Issuers or Their Affiliates").

*   *   *

Here, the plaintiffs allege that the Director Defendants had a disqualifying self-interest because they were financially motivated to maintain the status quo. A claim of this kind must be viewed with caution, because to argue that directors have an entrenchment motive solely because they could lose their positions following an acquisition is, to an extent, tautological. By its very nature, a board decision to reject a merger proposal could always enable a plaintiff to assert that a majority of the directors had an entrenchment motive. For that reason, the plaintiffs must plead, in addition to a motive to retain corporate control, other facts sufficient to state a cognizable claim that the Director Defendants acted disloyally.[6]

The plaintiffs have done that here. At the time the Sales Process was terminated, the Board members were Stephens, Kramer, Eddy, Zuzolo and Gander. Only Gander voted to accept the First Place merger bid. The pled facts are sufficient to establish disloyalty of at least three (*i.e.*, a majority) of the remaining directors, which suffices to rebut the business judgment presumption. First, the Reclassification Proxy itself admits that the Company's directors and officers had "a conflict of interest with respect to [the Reclassification] because he or she is in a position to structure it in a way that benefits his or her interests differently from the interest of the unaffiliated stockholders." Second, a director-specific analysis establishes (for Rule 12(b)(6) purposes) that a majority of the Board was conflicted.

Stephens: Aside from Stephens losing his long held positions as President, Chairman and CEO of First Niles and the Bank, the plaintiffs have alleged specific conduct from which a duty of loyalty violation can reasonably be inferred. Stephens never responded to Cortland's due diligence request. The Financial Advisor noted that Stephens' failure to respond had caused Cortland to withdraw its bid. Even after Cortland had offered First Niles an extension, Stephens did not furnish the necessary due diligence materials, nor did he inform the Board of these due diligence problems until after Cortland withdrew. Cortland had also explicitly stated in its bid letter that the incumbent Board would be terminated if Cortland acquired First Niles. From these alleged facts it may reasonably be inferred that what motivated Stephens' unexplained failure to respond promptly to Cortland's due diligence request was his personal financial interest, as opposed to the interests of the shareholders. That same inference can be drawn from Stephens' response to the First Place bid: Count I alleges that Stephens attempted to "sabotage" the First Place due diligence request in a manner similar to what occurred with Cortland.

---

[6]   See Pogostin v. Rice, 480 A.2d 619, 627 (Del. 1984), *overruled on other grounds by Brehm v. Eisner*, 746 A.2d 244 (Del. 2000) ("plaintiffs have failed to plead any facts supporting their claim[s] that the ... board rejected the ... offer solely to retain control. Rather, plaintiffs seek to establish a motive or primary purpose to retain control only by showing that the ... board opposed a tender offer. Acceptance of such an argument would condemn any board, which successfully avoided a takeover, regardless of whether that board properly determined that it was acting in the best interests of the shareholders.").

Thus, the pled facts provide a sufficient basis to conclude, for purposes of a Rule 12(b)(6) motion to dismiss, that Stephens acted disloyally.

Kramer: Director Kramer's alleged circumstances establish a similar disqualifying conflict. Kramer was the President of William Kramer & Son, a heating and air conditioning company in Niles that provided heating and air conditioning services to the Bank. It is reasonable to infer that Kramer feared that if the Company were sold his firm would lose the Bank as a client. The loss of such a major client would be economically significant, because the complaint alleges that Kramer was a man of comparatively modest means, and that his company had few major assets and was completely leveraged. Because Kramer would suffer significant injury to his personal business interest if the Sales Process went forward, those pled facts are sufficient to support a reasonable inference that Kramer disloyally voted to terminate the Sales Process and support the Privatization Proposal.

Zuzolo: As earlier noted, Director Zuzolo was a principal in a small law firm in Niles that frequently provided legal services to First Niles and the Bank. Zuzolo was also the sole owner of a real estate title company that provided title services in nearly all of Home Federal's real estate transactions. Because Zuzolo, like Kramer, had a strong personal interest in having the Sales Process not go forward, the same reasonable inferences that flow from Kramer's personal business interest can be drawn in Zuzolo's case.

In summary, the plaintiffs have alleged facts sufficient to establish, for purposes of a motion to dismiss, that a majority of the First Niles Board acted disloyally. Because a cognizable claim of disloyalty rebuts the business judgment presumption, we need not reach the separate question of whether, in deciding to terminate the Sales Process, the Director Defendants acted advisedly (*i.e.*, with due care). Because the claim of disloyalty was subject to entire fairness review, the Court of Chancery erred in dismissing Count I as to the Director Defendants on the basis of the business judgment presumption.[7]

---

[7]   The Court of Chancery determined that entire fairness review was inappropriate, because: (1) it would be problematic to determine "fair price" without a completed transaction, (2) the Board did not interpose itself between the shareholders and a potential acquirer by implementing any defensive measures, and (3) entire fairness review would be inconsistent with Delaware's broad allocation to power to directors. *See Gander v. Stephens*, 2008 Del. Ch. LEXIS 20, 2008 WL 401124, at *9-10 (Del. Ch. February 14, 2008). Although it may be problematic to determine the fair price of a transaction that was never finalized, our decisions have applied the entire fairness standard in a non-transaction context. *See Nixon v. Blackwell*, 626 A.2d 1366, 1376 (Del. 1993) (applying the fair dealing prong of entire fairness). That the Board did not implement any impermissible defensive measures does not, *ipso facto*, insulate their actions from entire fairness review. Nor does Delaware's broad allocation of power to directors require less searching review where shareholders are able to establish a cognizable claim of self-interested director behavior.

*   *   *

III.   The Court of Chancery Erroneously Dismissed Count III of the Complaint

Finally, we address the issues generated by the dismissal of Count III. That Count alleges that the defendants breached their duty of loyalty by recommending the Reclassification Proposal to the shareholders for purely self-interested reasons (to enlarge their ability to engage in stock buy-backs and to trigger their ESOP put and appraisal rights).   *   *   * The Vice Chancellor then concluded that the complaint sufficiently alleged that a majority of the directors that approved the Reclassification Proposal lacked independence. Despite having so concluded, the court dismissed the claim on the ground that a disinterested majority of the shareholders had "ratified" the Reclassification by voting to approve it.

The plaintiffs claim that this ratification ruling is erroneous as a matter of law. They argue that because the Proxy disclosures were materially misleading, no fully informed shareholder vote took place. The plaintiffs also urge that in determining the number of unaffiliated shares that were voted, the Court of Chancery took improper judicial notice of shares owned by the defendants. The defendants respond that the Vice Chancellor's ratification ruling is correct and should be upheld. Alternatively, they argue that we should overturn the Vice Chancellor's determination that the Board had a disqualifying self-interest.

We conclude that the Court of Chancery legally erred in upholding Count III on shareholder ratification grounds, for two reasons. First, because a shareholder vote was required to amend the certificate of incorporation, that approving vote could not also operate to "ratify" the challenged conduct of the interested directors. Second, the adjudicated cognizable claim that the Reclassification Proxy contained a material misrepresentation, eliminates an essential predicate for applying the doctrine, namely, that the shareholder vote was fully informed.

A. The Doctrine of Shareholder Ratification

Under current Delaware case law, the scope and effect of the common law doctrine of shareholder ratification is unclear, making it difficult to apply that doctrine in a coherent manner. As the Court of Chancery has noted in *In re Wheelabrator Technologies, Inc., Shareholder Litigation*:

> The doctrine of ratification] might be thought to lack coherence because the decisions addressing the effect of shareholder "ratification" have fragmented that subject into three distinct compartments, ... In its "classic" ... form, shareholder ratification describes the situation where shareholders approve board action that, legally speaking, could be accomplished without any shareholder approval.... "[C]lassic" ratification involves the voluntary addition of an independent layer of shareholder approval in circumstances where shareholder approval is not legally required. But "shareholder ratification" has also been used to describe the

effect of an informed shareholder vote that was statutorily required for the transaction to have legal existence.... That [the Delaware courts] have used the same term is such highly diverse sets of factual circumstances, without regard to their possible functional differences, suggests that "shareholder ratification" has now acquired an expanded meaning intended to describe any approval of challenged board action by a fully informed vote of shareholders, irrespective of whether that shareholder vote is legally required for the transaction to attain legal existence.[52]

To restore coherence and clarity to this area of our law, we hold that the scope of the shareholder ratification doctrine must be limited to its so-called "classic" form; that is, to circumstances where a fully informed shareholder vote approves director action that does *not* legally require shareholder approval in order to become legally effective. Moreover, the only director action or conduct that can be ratified is that which the shareholders are specifically asked to approve. With one exception, the "cleansing" effect of such a ratifying shareholder vote is to subject the challenged director action to business judgment review, as opposed to "extinguishing" the claim altogether (*i.e.*, obviating all judicial review of the challenged action).[54]

B.   Applying the Doctrine to the Shareholders' Approval of the

---

[52]   663 A.2d 1194, 1202 and n.4 (Del. Ch. 1995) (citations omitted). *See also Solomon v. Armstrong*, 747 A.2d 1098, 1114-15 (Del. Ch. 1999), *aff'd*, 746 A.2d 277 (Table) ("The legal effect of shareholder ratification, as it relates to alleged breaches of the duty of loyalty, may be one of the most tortured areas of Delaware law. A different rule exists for every permutation of facts that fall under the broad umbrella of "duty of loyalty" claims.").

[54]   To the extent that *Smith v. Van Gorkom* holds otherwise, it is overruled. 488 A.2d 858, 889-90 (Del. 1985). The only species of claim that shareholder ratification can validly extinguish is a claim that the directors lacked the authority to take action that was later ratified. Nothing herein should be read as altering the well-established principle that void acts such as fraud, gift, waste and ultra vires acts cannot be ratified by a less than unanimous shareholder vote. *See Michelson v. Duncan*, 407 A.2d 211, 219 (Del. 1979) ("[W]here a claim of gift or waste of assets, fraud or [u]ltra vires is asserted that a less than unanimous shareholder ratification is not a full defense."); *see also Harbor Fin. Partners v. Huizenga*, 751 A.2d 879, 896 (Del. Ch. 1999) (explaining that ultra vires, fraud, and gift or waste of corporate assets are "void" acts that cannot be ratified by less than unanimous shareholder consent.) *accord Solomon v. Armstrong*, 747 A.2d at 1115. "Voidable" acts are those beyond management's powers, but where they are performed in the best interests of the corporation they may be ratified by a majority vote of disinterested shareholders. *See Michelson*, 407 A.2d at 219.

To avoid confusion about the doctrinal clarifications set forth in Part III A of this Opinion, we note that they apply only to the common law doctrine of shareholder ratification. They are not intended to affect or alter our jurisprudence governing the effect of an approving vote of disinterested shareholders under 8 *Del. C.* § 144.

Reclassification Proposal

The Court of Chancery held that although Count III of the complaint pled facts establishing that the Reclassification Proposal was an interested transaction not entitled to business judgment protection, the shareholders' fully informed vote "ratifying" that Proposal reinstated the business judgment presumption. That ruling was legally erroneous, for several reasons. First, the ratification doctrine does not apply to transactions where shareholder approval is statutorily required. Here, the Reclassification could not become legally effective without a statutorily mandated shareholder vote approving the amendment to First Niles' certificate of incorporation. Second, because we have determined that the complaint states a cognizable claim that the Reclassification Proxy was materially misleading (*see* Part II, *supra*, of this Opinion), that precludes ruling at this procedural juncture, as a matter of law, that the Reclassification was fully informed. Therefore, the approving shareholder vote did not operate as a "ratification" of the challenged conduct in any legally meaningful sense.[55]

Alternatively, the defendants urge that, apart from ratification, Count III was properly dismissed because the Board was not interested, and that the Vice Chancellor's contrary ruling is erroneous. That argument lacks merit both procedurally and substantively. Procedurally it lacks merit because the Court of Chancery expressly determined that a majority of the Board was interested, and the Defendants have not cross-appealed from that ruling. Substantively, the argument lacks merit, because the defendants concede that Stephens and Csontos were interested in the Reclassification, and our earlier analysis of Kramer's alleged disloyalty with respect to Count I applies equally to Count III. These allegations require that the Vice Chancellor's determination that a majority of the Board was interested be sustained.

We conclude that the Court of Chancery erroneously dismissed Count III of the complaint.

CONCLUSION

For the foregoing reasons, the judgment of the Court of Chancery is reversed as to all counts and remanded for proceedings consistent with the rulings in this Opinion.

Question:

1.   Assume that the Arledge and Chiteia memo had been disclosed to the UOP

---

[55]   We have previously suggested this result in *Williams v. Geier*, 671 A.2d 1368, 1379 n.24 (Del. 1996) (dictum). This Opinion clarifies that "ratification" legally describes only corporate action where stockholder approval is not statutorily required for its effectuation.

stockholders in the proxy materials, with an admission that it had been withheld from the UOP board, and that the details of the "negotiations" had been discussed more fully. Would this have permitted the UOP stockholder vote for the merger to ratify the earlier wrongful act under the *Gantler* rule?

2.   Does this decision require separate votes on ratification and on the amendments to the certificate of incorporation?

3.   Suppose the proxy statement contained separate proposals (1) to ratify the directors' conflicted actions in proposing the classification and (2) approving the amendments to the certificate of incorporation, and that the independent shareholders voted against proposition (1) and for proposition (2). What result?

Add on 865, in place of In Re Tele-Communications, Inc. Shareholders Litigation:

In Re John Q. Hammons Hotels Inc. Shareholder Litigation

2009 Del. Ch. LEXIS 174

CHANDLER, Chancellor

This case arises out of the merger in September of 2005 of John Q. Hammons Hotels, Inc. ("JQH" or the "Company") with and into an acquisition vehicle indirectly owned by Jonathan Eilian, pursuant to which the holders of JQH Class A common stock received $ 24 per share in cash (the "Merger"). Plaintiffs in this purported class action seek damages for the allegedly inadequate price paid for the publicly held Class A shares. Plaintiffs contend that John Q. Hammons, JQH's controlling stockholder, used his control position to negotiate an array of private benefits for himself that were not shared with the minority stockholders. Eilian, a third party with no prior relationship with Hammons or JQH, negotiated with Hammons and the special committee, which was formed to represent and negotiate on behalf of the minority stockholders. The result of these negotiations was that the Class A stockholders received cash for their shares, and Hammons, in exchange for his Class B stock and interest in a limited partnership controlled by JQH, received a small equity interest in the surviving limited partnership, a preferred interest with a large liquidation preference, and various other contractual rights and obligations.

Plaintiffs contend that Hammons breached his fiduciary duties as a controlling stockholder by negotiating benefits for himself that were not shared with the minority stockholders. Plaintiffs also contend that the JQH directors breached their fiduciary duties by allowing the Merger to be negotiated through an allegedly deficient process, and by voting to approve the Merger. Plaintiffs also assert claims against the Merger acquisition vehicles for aiding and abetting the breaches of fiduciary duty. Finally, plaintiffs assert four disclosure claims based on alleged misstatements and omissions in the Company's proxy statement.

Before the Court are cross-motions for summary judgment, and the threshold issue is <u>whether the Court should apply the entire fairness or business</u> <u>judgment standard of review.</u> Defendants argue that business judgment is the appropriate standard of review because (1) Hammons was not involved in the process of negotiation for the purchase of the minority shares, (2) the minority stockholders were adequately represented by the disinterested and independent special committee, and (3) a majority of the minority stockholders approved the Merger in a fully informed vote. Plaintiffs, of course, disagree, and contend that entire fairness is the appropriate standard of review because (1) the special committee was ineffective, (2) the majority of the minority vote was "illusory," and (3) Hammons was subject to a conflict of interest because he negotiated benefits for himself that were not shared with the minority stockholders. Plaintiffs assert that the minority stockholders were "coerced" into accepting the Merger because the price of the Class A stock did not reflect the Company's true value. Moreover, according to plaintiffs, Hammons's ability to block any transaction limited the special committee's ability to negotiate at arm's length and relegated it to the subservient role of negotiating only with bidders acceptable to Hammons.

As explained below, I conclude that Kahn v. Lynch Communication Systems, Inc. does not mandate application of the entire fairness standard of review in this case, notwithstanding any procedural protections that may have been used. Rather, the use of sufficient procedural protections for the minority stockholders *could* have resulted in application of the business judgment standard of review in this case. The procedures used here, however, were not sufficient to invoke business judgment review. Accordingly, the appropriate standard of review is entire fairness. As explained below, defendants' motions for summary judgment are granted in part and denied in part, and plaintiffs' motion for summary judgment is granted in part and denied in part.

I.   BACKGROUND

A.   The Parties

Defendant JQH was a Delaware corporation headquartered in Springfield, Missouri that engaged in the business of owning and managing hotels. JQH owned forty-four hotels and managed another fifteen. Most of the hotels were franchised under major trade names, such as Embassy Suites Hotels, Holiday Inn, and Marriott, and located in or near a stable "demand generator" such as a state capital, university, convention center, corporate headquarters, or office park.

<u>JQH was formed in 1994, and used the proceeds from its initial public stock</u> <u>offering to purchase an approximately 28% general partnership interest in John Q.</u> <u>Hammons Hotels, LP ("JQHLP"). Hammons owned the remaining 72% of JQHLP</u> <u>as its sole limited partner.</u> JQH conducted its business operations through JQHLP.

Ownership of JQH was held through two classes of stock. The Class A common stock was publicly traded and entitled to one vote per share. The Class B common stock was not publicly traded and was entitled to fifty votes per share.

Hammons and his affiliates owned approximately 5% of the Class A common stock and all of the Class B common stock. Thus, Hammons had approximately 76% of the total vote in JQH, which in turn controlled JQHLP as its sole general partner. Plaintiffs Jolly Roger Fund, LP, Jolly Roger Offshore Fund, Ltd., and Lemon Bay Partners were purported owners of Class A common stock.

The JQH Board of Directors (the "Board") was composed of eight members at the time of the Merger. Hammons was Chairman of the Board and Chief Executive Officer. The other Board members were John E. Lopez-Ona, Daniel L. Earley, William J. Hart, David C. Sullivan, Donald H. Dempsey, James F. Moore, and Jacqueline A. Dowdy.

Defendants JQH Acquisition, LLC ("Acquisition") and JQH Merger Corporation ("Merger Sub") were formed to facilitate the Merger. Eilian is the principal of Acquisition. Merger Sub is a wholly owned subsidiary of Acquisition.

B.   The Company and Hammons Before the Merger

The price of JQH Class A shares declined after the initial public offering at $ 16.50 per share, and, according to plaintiffs, eventually traded in the $ 4 to $ 7 range until sometime in 2004, when rumors of a possible merger first circulated. Plaintiffs suggest that low stock price could have resulted from the small number of publicly traded shares, the lack of an active trading market in those shares, the lack of any meaningful analyst coverage, and the lack of large institutional investors. Plaintiffs also contend that the shares were "burdened" by the presence of a large controlling stockholder, and that Hammons's self-dealing depressed the price of the Class A shares.

Hammons's passion was, and is, developing hotels, and Hammons took pride in the quality of his hotels. Hammons was seen by many as a legend in the hotel business, as evidenced by his biography, *They Call Him John Q.: A Hotel Legend.* It also appears, however, that the relationship between Hammons and the Board was, at least at times, tense.

Plaintiffs cite evidence and quote from Hammons's biography for the proposition that Hammons only reluctantly sold shares in JQH to the public, that he disliked the procedural requirements associated with public stockholders and a board of directors, and that there was tension between Hammons and the Board. Indeed, Hammons and the Board had disagreements over the Board's use of stock options as compensation and over the pace of hotel development. The latter disagreement resulted in the Board's call for a moratorium on the development of hotels by the Company. This moratorium led the Board and Hammons to negotiate an arrangement where Hammons was permitted to use Company resources for his private development activities, in exchange for giving the Company the opportunity to manage such hotels and acquire them if they were offered for sale.

Hammons and the Board also disagreed over Hammons's decision to offer Lou Weckstein, who Hammons hired as JQH's President in 2001 without consulting the Board, a salary that the Board believed was excessive. This conflict led to deterioration of the relationship between Hammons and Hart, who was then Hammons's personal attorney, and led the Board to retain Katten Muchin Rosenman, LLP ("Katten Muchin") to advise the non-employee members of the Board on how to react to Hammons's hiring of Weckstein.

Plaintiffs point to Eilian's description in a March 7, 2005 email sent during the negotiations that Hammons practiced a "'liberal' mixing of private and personal expenses and competitive interests." In its 2004 10-K the Company disclosed that:

> Mr. Hammons also (1) owns hotels that we manage; (2) owns an interest in a hotel management company that provides accounting and other administrative services for all of our hotels; (3) owns a 50% interest in the entity from which we lease our corporate headquarters; (4) has an agreement whereby we pay up to 1.5% of his internal development costs for new hotels in exchange for the opportunity to manage the hotels and the right of first refusal to purchase the hotels in the event they are offered for sale; (5) leases space to us in two trade centers owned by him that connect with two of our hotels; (6) has the right to require the redemption of his LP Units; (7) utilizes our administration and other services for his outside business interests, for which he reimburses us; (8) utilizes the services of certain of our employees in his personal enterprises and personally subsidizes those employees' compensation; and (9) owns the real estate underlying one of our hotels, which we lease from him.

Plaintiffs also point to a conflict surrounding rent the Company paid to Hammons for meeting space adjacent to one of the Company's hotels in Portland, Oregon. Plaintiffs cite evidence that, according to Weckstein and Paul Muellner, JQH's chief financial officer, Hammons insisted on a rent well in excess of market rates and opposed the lower rental offer they proposed.

Around early 2004, Hammons and the Board also had conflicts over the plan to dispose of certain Holiday Inn hotels that the Board and management (other than Hammons) deemed were no longer "core assets" of the Company. Hammons, who Muellner described as having an "emotional attachment" to the Holiday Inn brand, opposed the sale of some of the hotels and even threatened to take legal action to stop the Board from selling one of the properties. On a separate occasion, without disclosure to the Board, Hammons entered into a private agreement with a listing broker that gave Hammons a right of first refusal, which would have allowed Hammons to match an offer in the event a third-party offer was approved by the Board. The arrangement was later discovered and disclosed to the Board by the Company's general counsel.

C.   The Barcelo Offer and the Creation of the Special Committee

In early 2004, Hammons informed the Board that he had begun discussions with third parties regarding a potential sale of JQH or his interest in JQH. On October 15, 2004, one of these third parties, Barcelo Crestline Corporation

("Barcelo"), informed the Board that it had entered into an agreement with Hammons and that it was offering $ 13 per share for all outstanding shares of JQH Class A common stock.

The agreement Barcelo reached with Hammons reflected Hammons's tax and other personal objectives. Hammons's tax situation made it essential to him that any transaction be structured to avoid the large tax liability that would result from a transaction that was deemed to be a disposition event for Hammons. To accomplish this goal, Hammons had to retain some ownership in the surviving limited partnership and continue to have capital at risk. Hammons also desired, among other things, a line of credit that would allow him to continue to develop hotels. Thus, the deal announced by Barcelo was structured such that in exchange for his interests in JQH and JQHLP, Hammons would receive a small ownership percentage in Barcelo's acquisition vehicle and a preferred interest with a large liquidation preference. The Barcelo transaction also provided that Hammons would receive a line of credit of up to $ 250 million and distribution of Chateau on the Lake Resort (the "Chateau Lake property"), one of JQH's premier properties.

Recognizing that Hammons's interests in the transaction may not have been identical to those of the unaffiliated JQH stockholders, the Board formed a special committee to evaluate and negotiate a proposed transaction on behalf of the unaffiliated stockholders and make a recommendation to the Board. The special committee consisted of Sullivan, Dempsey, and Moore. Discussions at the initial meetings of the special committee in October 2004 reveal that the members realized that the special committee lacked the ability to broadly market the Company in light of Hammons's controlling interest and ability to reject any transaction. Thus, the special committee determined that its goal was to pursue the best price reasonably available to minority stockholders in any transaction the special committee was authorized to consider. The special committee also recognized its duty to recommend against a transaction if the committee concluded that the transaction was not in the best interests of the minority stockholders or if the price offered to the minority stockholders was not fair, from a financial perspective, to the minority stockholders. On the advice of its counsel, the special committee also adopted guidelines that provided that the special committee would conduct a process in which (1) stockholders would be provided a reasonable opportunity to express their views to the committee, (2) all parties interested and willing to explore a transaction would be afforded a level playing field, from the Company's perspective, on which to pursue a transaction in terms of timing and access to information, and (3) the committee and its advisors would be fully informed as to the value, merits, and probability of closing any transaction that there was a reasonable basis for believing could be consummated. The special committee retained Katten Muchin as its legal advisor and Lehman Brothers ("Lehman") as its financial advisor.

The special committee also discussed that, after Barcelo's public announcement, Eilian had contacted members of the special committee and told them he was interested in entering into a possible transaction with the Company.

Eilian indicated that Hammons had suggested that he contact the special committee if he felt he could offer a proposal superior to Barcelo's. The special committee agreed that its counsel would contact Eilian and inform him that Lehman had been retained as the special committee's financial advisor.

Although Barcelo's agreement with Hammons expired by its terms on November 1, 2004, both Barcelo and Hammons remained interested in going forward with the transaction pursuant to a new agreement. On November 16, 2004, the Board (with Hammons abstaining) expanded the authority of the special committee to review, evaluate, and negotiate on behalf of the unaffiliated stockholders the terms of the revised Barcelo proposal. The Board also gave the special committee the authority to respond to, and act on behalf of the board with respect to, any requests from interested parties.

On December 5, 2004, following a November 18, 2004 meeting with the special committee, Eilian submitted a proposal to the special committee whereby his group would acquire the interests of Hammons in the Company and make a tender offer for the unaffiliated stockholders at a price to be determined.[5] In November, the special committee met with various shareholder groups, including representatives of plaintiffs.

On December 6, 2004, the special committee reviewed the outstanding proposals of Barcelo and Eilian. After receiving a preliminary evaluation from Lehman that Barcelo's $ 13 per share offer was inadequate, from a financial point of view, to the minority stockholders, the special committee unanimously agreed to recommend to the Board that it reject Barcelo's revised agreement with Hammons. The next day, the special committee advised the Board that Barcelo's offer was not acceptable, and the Company issued a press release stating that the Company would not accept the Barcelo proposal.

At a December 23, 2004 meeting, two special committee members reported that A.G. Edwards had contacted them on behalf of Eagle Hospitality Properties Trust, Inc. ("Eagle"). The committee, after observing that Eagle would need to raise significant capital, that a transaction with Eagle would involve a significant amount of strategic and financial risks, and that there was no basis to believe that Hammons would have any interest in pursuing a transaction with Eagle, concluded that the

---

[5]   Although the special committee had indicated that it would seek to provide "a level playing field" in terms of access to information, the special committee determined at a November 30, 2004 meeting that it would not place JQH management in a "tenuous position" by overriding Hammons's instruction to JQH's general counsel not to send due diligence materials to Eilian at that time. Hammons had expressed that he would not do a deal with Eilian under any circumstances. Nevertheless, the special committee attempted to encourage Eilian and his advisors to not let Hammons's instruction dissuade them from continuing to evaluate a possible transaction and maintaining an open dialogue with the Company's financial advisor.

inquiry from Eagle was not worth pursuing at that point in time.

By December 28, 2004, Barcelo was willing to pay $ 21 per share of Class A common stock if the transaction was subject to approval by a simple majority of shares, including those owned by Hammons. Barcelo was willing to pay only $ 20 per share if a separate majority of the minority vote was required. Eilian's proposed transaction with a tender offer for the Class A shares of at least $ 20.50 per share had been outlined to the special committee on December 23, 2004. At the December 28 meeting, the special committee discussed both proposals and concluded that the Barcelo proposal was more fully negotiated and stood a far greater chance of being consummated.

At a December 29, 2004 meeting, the special committee was informed that Barcelo was willing to increase its offer to acquire the Class A stock to $ 21 per share and agree that any merger be conditioned on a majority vote of the unaffiliated stockholders. Lehman advised the special committee that the $ 21 per share offer was fair to the minority stockholders from a financial point of view and that the allocation of consideration between the minority stockholders and Hammons was reasonable.

At a Board meeting later that day, the special committee advised the Board of Barcelo's revised proposal as well as the proposal from Eilian's group that would offer $ 20.50 per share for all Class A shares. Hammons indicated that he was no longer interested in a transaction with Eilian. Based on the special committee's recommendation, the Board resolved to provide Barcelo with exclusivity until January 31, 2005.

Negotiations proceeded between Barcelo and Hammons, but Hammons was ultimately not comfortable with the proposal, particularly because he believed that the three-year commitment on the line of credit was not sufficient. An agreement was not reached by January 31, and Hammons indicated that he was unwilling to extend exclusivity with Barcelo. The special committee then recommended to the Board that the Company not renew exclusivity with Barcelo, and the Board followed this recommendation.

D.   The Eilian Offer

On January 31, 2005, the special committee received an offer from Eilian's group by which Acquisition would acquire all outstanding Class A common stock for $ 24 per share. Eilian's letter to the special committee indicated that the offer was not contingent on third-party financing and that certain Class A stockholders unaffiliated with Hammons had entered into agreements pursuant to which those stockholders agreed to support Eilian's proposal.[6] The committee informed the Board of this offer, and the Board voted to continue the existence and authorization

---

[6]   According to defendants, these unaffiliated stockholders represented approximately 23% of the public Class A common stockholders.

of the special committee.

At a February 3, 2005 Board meeting, Hammons informed the Board that he would like to negotiate a transaction with Eilian. At the same meeting, the Board was informed that the Company had received an expression of interest from Eagle and from Corporex Companies. The Board concluded that because Eagle and Corporex did not come forward sooner after the expiration of the exclusivity period with Barcelo and because of many other factors discussed at the meeting, the Board would not pursue a transaction with that group and would instead proceed expeditiously to negotiate a transaction with Eilian. Based upon a recommendation from the special committee, the Board granted Eilian exclusivity until February 28, 2005.

Over the next several months, representatives of Eilian, Hammons, and the special committee continued to negotiate the terms of a potential deal, during which time the exclusivity agreement with Elian was renewed several times. On June 3, 2005, Hammons and Acquisition (Eilian's acquisition vehicle) informed the special committee that they had reached certain agreements and requested the special committee's approval of them. Acquisition also reaffirmed its offer to purchase all the outstanding shares of Class A common stock held by unaffiliated stockholders for $ 24 per share.

On June 14, 2005, the special committee met with its advisors. Katten Muchin reviewed the process the special committee used over the previous nine months and provided an overview of the various agreements between Hammons and Acquisition. Lehman provided a presentation of its analysis and methodology in issuing its fairness opinion that the $ 24 per share price was fair to the minority stockholders from a financial point of view. Lehman also advised the special committee of its opinion that the allocation of the consideration between Hammons and the unaffiliated stockholders was reasonable. Lehman calculated that the value received by Hammons and his affiliates was between $ 11.95 and $ 14.74 per share. The special committee then approved the merger agreement (the "Merger Agreement") and the related agreements between Hammons and Eilian (collectively with the Merger Agreement, the "Transaction Agreements").

The Board met immediately following the June 14 special committee meeting. Hammons advised the Board that he supported the proposed transactions and then recused himself from the meeting. After presentations from Katten Muchin on the Transaction Agreements and the Board's fiduciary duties, and from Lehman on its fairness opinion, the Board voted to approve the Merger and the Transaction Agreements.

E. The Merger and the Transaction Agreements

The Merger Agreement provided that each share of Class A common stock would be converted into the right to receive $ 24 per share in cash upon consummation of the Merger. The Merger was contingent on approval by a majority of the unaffiliated Class A stockholders, unless that requirement was waived by the special committee.[7] The Merger Agreement included a termination fee of up to $ 20 million and a "no shop" provision that placed limitations on the Company's ability to solicit offers from other parties. Moreover, Hammons agreed to vote his interests in favor of the Merger and against any competing proposal or other action that would prevent or hinder the completion of the Merger.

In addition to the Merger Agreement, Hammons and Acquisition entered into a series of other agreements, which provided for a complex, multi-step transaction designed to provide Hammons financing to continue his hotel development activities without triggering the tax liability associated with an equity or asset sale. Although each Class B share initially remained a share of common stock of the surviving corporation, those shares were eventually converted into a preferred interest in the surviving limited partnership (the "surviving LP"). In order to achieve his tax goals, Hammons had to have an ownership interest in the surviving LP and continue to have capital at risk. Accordingly, Hammons was allocated a 2% interest in the cash flow distributions and preferred equity of the surviving LP. Atrium GP, LLC, an Eilian company, became general partner of the surviving LP and received a 98% ownership interest. Hammons's preexisting limited partner interest in JQHLP was converted into a capital account associated with his preferred interest in the surviving LP, which had a liquidation preference of $ 328 million. When combined with the preferred interest from the conversion of his Class B shares, Hammons's capital account totaled a liquidation preference of $ 335 million. The partnership agreement provided for events in which the capital account could be distributed during Hammons's lifetime, but because of certain tax consequences, it was anticipated that distribution of the capital account was to occur at Hammons's death.

The terms of the Transaction Agreements also provided Hammons other rights and obligations. Importantly, Hammons received a $ 25 million short-term line of credit and a $ 275 million long-term line of credit. Hammons also received (1) the Company's Chateau Lake property in exchange for transferring certain assets and related liabilities to an Acquisition affiliate, (2) a right of first refusal to acquire hotels sold post-merger, and (3) an indemnification agreement for any tax liability from the surviving LP's sale of any of its hotels during Hammons's lifetime. Hammons and Eilian entered into a reciprocal agreement that imposed restrictions on the development of new hotels that would compete with existing hotels owned by either party. Hammons also obtained an agreement whereby his management entity would continue to manage the hotels in exchange for payments of actual operating costs and expenses incurred (estimated to be approximately $ 6.5 million based on the budget for 2005) and a $ 200,000 annual salary to Hammons, plus

---

[7]   As explained below, plaintiffs discount the majority of the minority vote because it only required approval of a majority of the minority shares voting, as opposed to a majority of all the minority shares.

benefits. [9]

On August 24, 2005, the Company sent a proxy statement to its stockholders in connection with the vote on the Merger at a special meeting of stockholders on September 15, 2005. Of the 5,253,262 issued and outstanding shares of Class A stock, 3,821,005 shares, or over 72%, were voted to approve the Merger. In total, more than 89% of the Class A shares that voted on the Merger voted to approve it. The Merger closed on September 16, 2005.

F. Plaintiffs' Contentions Regarding the Negotiation Process

Plaintiffs paint a picture of the negotiation process that is dominated by Hammons's ability to walk away and block any transaction, which would have left plaintiffs holding illiquid stock that would likely trade in the $ 4 to $ 7 range. According to plaintiffs, this threat relegated the special committee to a passive, tag-along role and forced them to be "friends of the deal" in an effort to prevent Hammons from backing out of the deal.

*   *   *

G. The Litigation

*   *   * The director defendants seek summary judgment on the grounds that (1) plaintiffs cannot satisfy their burden to rebut the presumption of the business judgment rule, (2) the special committee members and the director defendants are shielded from monetary liability pursuant to the Company's 8 Del. C. § 102(b)(7) exculpatory provision, and (3) there is no evidence to support the aiding and abetting claim. *   *   * Plaintiffs seek summary judgment holding that (1) entire fairness is the applicable standard of review, (2) the special committee process and stockholder vote were ineffective and the burden of persuasion at trial remains with defendants, (3) the challenged transactions were the result of unfair dealing, (4) certain defendants are liable for aiding and abetting Hammons's breach, and (5) the only issue for trial is therefore fair price. Plaintiffs now concede that Revlon, Inc. v. MacAndrews & Forbes Holdings, Inc. does not govern the duties of the Board, that the special committee was disinterested and independent (although not free from coercion by Hammons), and that a number of the disclosure violations previously alleged should be withdrawn.

II. ANALYSIS

*   *   *

B. The Standard of Review: Entire Fairness or Business Judgment?

The threshold issue is whether the Court should apply the entire fairness

---

[9]   Hammons apparently had high standards for his hotels, and took pride in his organization's reputation for quality products. The management agreement allowed Hammons to ensure the hotels were maintained to his standards.

standard or the business judgment standard in reviewing the Merger. Plaintiffs label the Merger a "minority squeeze-out transaction" and contend that Kahn v. Lynch Communication Systems, Inc. mandates that the Court apply the entire fairness standard of review, while defendants urge the Court to apply the business judgment standard of review.

In Lynch the Delaware Supreme Court held "that the exclusive standard of judicial review in examining the propriety of an interested cash-out merger transaction by a controlling or dominating shareholder is entire fairness" and that "[t]he initial burden of establishing entire fairness rests upon the party who stands on both sides of the transaction." Additionally, "approval of the transaction by an independent committee of directors or an informed majority of minority shareholders" would shift the burden of proof on the issue of fairness to the plaintiff, but would not change that entire fairness was the standard of review.[21]

Plaintiffs contend that Lynch controls this case and mandates application of the entire fairness standard, regardless of any procedural protections that were used that may have protected the minority stockholders. Plaintiffs argue that Hammons stood on both sides of the transaction because he did not in fact sell his interest in the companies to Eilian, but rather restructured them in a way that accomplished his tax and financing goals while maintaining a significant interest in the surviving company, in addition to other rights. Plaintiffs point not only to Hammons's numerous contractual arrangements and continuing preferred interest in the surviving LP, but also to statements from various witnesses that the transaction was not actually a "sale" by Hammons but rather a "joint venture of some sort" or a "recapitalization" designed to accomplish Hammons's tax and liquidity needs. Thus, plaintiffs contend:

> as viewed from a legal and tax standpoint, as communicated to employees and the public, and as understood by the transaction participants themselves, the Related Transactions effected a restructuring in which Mr. Hammons brought in a business partner and obtained access to financing while retaining most of his equity (in modified form), together with substantial upside from future growth of JQH, significant veto rights over future operations of the Company, and continued direct management of the Company's hotel properties. Under these circumstances, the rule of Lynch-- that "the exclusive standard of judicial review in examining the propriety of an interested cash-out merger transaction by a controlling or dominating shareholder is entire fairness,"--applies directly.

---

[21]   Id. A different standard applies to transactions that effectively cash out minority shareholders through a tender offer followed by a short-form merger. See In re Aquila Inc., 805 A.2d 184, 190-91 (Del. Ch. 2002); In re Siliconix Inc. S'holders Litig., 2001 Del. Ch. LEXIS 83, 2001 WL 716787, at *6-9 (Del. Ch. June 21, 2001); see generally In re Pure Res., Inc. S'holders Litig., 808 A.2d 421, 434-39 (Del. Ch. 2002).

Although plaintiffs' argument has some appeal, ultimately, I disagree. Unlike in Lynch, the controlling stockholder in this case did not make the offer to the minority stockholders; an unrelated third party did. Eilian had no prior relationship with the Company or with Hammons. Eilian negotiated separately with Hammons, who had a right to sell (or refuse to sell) his shares, and with the minority stockholders, through the disinterested and independent special committee. The rights Hammons retained after the Merger--the 2% interest in the surviving LP, the preferred interest with a $335 million liquidation preference, and various other contractual rights and obligations--do not change that _Eilian_ made an offer to the minority stockholders, who were represented by the disinterested and independent special committee. Put simply, this case is not one in which Hammons stood "on both sides of the transaction." Accordingly, Lynch does not mandate that the entire fairness standard of review apply notwithstanding any procedural protections that were used.

Plaintiffs further contend that, even if Hammons did not stand on both sides of the transaction as contemplated in Lynch, the policy rationales underlying the _Lynch_ decision warrant extending its holding to this case. In support of this position, plaintiffs cite several Court of Chancery decisions in which the Court applied or extended Lynch. Although I do not fully address all the cases plaintiffs cite in support of this argument, I generally reach two conclusions with respect to them: first, the cases plaintiffs cite can be factually distinguished from this case, and second, to the extent those cases extended the application of Lynch based on certain policy rationales, I decline to do so here.

[handwritten margin note: Doesn't agree w/ JC]

For example, in In re Tele-Communications, Inc. Shareholders Litigation,[25] the evidence suggested that a majority of the board of directors was interested because they received material personal benefits from the transaction they approved. Specifically, the transaction materially benefited a majority of the directors because it allocated a disproportionate amount of the merger consideration to the directors' class of stock. Moreover, only one of those directors was a controlling stockholder entitled to a control premium. Thus, the interestedness of a majority of the directors led the Court to apply the entire fairness standard and to conclude that, as in Lynch, the approval of the transaction by the stockholders and a special committee could at most shift the burden of demonstrating entire fairness to plaintiffs.[29] Here, in contrast, Hammons negotiated with Eilian and did not

---

[25]   2005 Del. Ch. LEXIS 206, 2005 WL 3642727 (Del. Ch. Dec. 21, 2005).

[29]   _Id._ at *8. Because of the conflict of interest of a majority of the board in that case, the Court in In re Telecommunications determined that entire fairness review should apply to the transaction. The Court also determined that, as in Lynch, approval by shareholders and a special committee could shift the burden of entire fairness to plaintiffs. Nothing in that case, however, suggests that such a rule must apply in every case in which the Court is determining whether to apply entire fairness review. In other words, the result in Lynch—that shareholder and special committee approval merely shifts the burden of entire fairness—does not

participate in the negotiations between Eilian and the special committee. Nothing in In re Tele-Communications mandates the extension of Lynch to this case.[30]

In In re LNR Property Corp. Shareholders Litigation,[31] the complaint alleged that the board breached its fiduciary duties by allowing a conflicted controlling shareholder, who was acting as both buyer and seller in the transaction, to "personally negotiate[] a one-sided deal that allowed him and select members of management to continue to reap the benefits of [the company's] future growth while cutting out plaintiff and the class."[32] The complaint also alleged that the controlling shareholder dominated and controlled the board and the "sham" special committee, which did not have the authority to engage in independent negotiations. Taking the allegations in the complaint in the light most favorable to plaintiffs, the Court could not, on a motion to dismiss, rule out the possibility that the entire fairness standard would apply because the controlling stockholder negotiated the transaction, including the allocation of a 20.4% stake in the resulting company for himself. The Court noted, however, that "[t]here is authority for the proposition that the mere fact that a controller has or may be acquiring some interest in the buyer does not automatically trigger entire fairness review." The Court noted that the business judgment standard of review may ultimately apply if, at a later stage, the defendants are able to show that the interests of the minority stockholders were adequately protected. As the *LNR Property* Court stated:

Of course, the defendants may be able to show at the summary

---

preclude the possibility that shareholder and special committee review could be relevant in determining whether to apply business judgment or entire fairness in a case that is not governed by Lynch.

[30]   Plaintiffs also cite In re Cysive, Inc. S'holders Litig., 836 A.2d 531 (Del. Ch. 2003) and In re W. Nat'l Corp. S'holders Litig., 2000 WL 710192 (Del. Ch. May 22, 2000). In Cysive, however, the Court addressed the question of whether the stockholder, who made the buy-out proposal to the minority stockholders, was a "controlling stockholder" for purposes of *Lynch*, and concluded that the large stockholder "possess[ed] the attributes of control that motivate the *Lynch* doctrine." Cysive, 836 A.2d at 551-552. In W. Nat'l, the plaintiff challenged the merger between Western National Corporation and its 46% stockholder. The Court concluded that the record did not support a finding of control. W. Nat'l at *5-10. Here, in contrast, there is no dispute that Hammons was the controlling stockholder of JQH. Hammons, however, did not make the offer to the minority stockholders or agree to a merger with JQH. Rather, an unaffiliated third-party negotiated separately with Hammons and the special committee.

[31]   896 A.2d 169 (Del. Ch. 2005).

[32]   Id. at 176. Similarly, in Ryan v. Tad's Enterprises, Inc., 709 A.2d 682 (Del. Ch. 1996) and In re Dairy Mart Convenience Stores, Inc., 1999 WL 350473 (Del. Ch. May 24, 1999), the Court applied entire fairness review where the controlling stockholder negotiated the transaction on behalf of the company and the minority stockholders.

judgment stage that Miller, as they argue, negotiated this transaction as a seller, not a buyer, and that the board and the Special Committee were entitled to repose confidence in his unconflicted motivation to obtain the maximum price for all LNR stockholders. In that case, the court may well be able to conclude that the measures taken by the board and the Special Committee to protect the interests of the minority were adequate in the circumstances to invoke the business judgment standard of review. Nonetheless, those facts and circumstances do not appear in the well pleaded allegations of the complaint.

Although I have determined that the measures taken in this case were not "adequate in the circumstances to invoke the business judgment standard of review," this result is not mandated by *Lynch*. Rather, it results from deficiencies in the specific procedures used in this case. In other words, I accept defendants' argument that *Lynch* does not mandate the application of entire fairness review in this case, notwithstanding any procedural protections for the minority stockholders.[37] In this case—which, again, I have determined is not governed by *Lynch*—business judgment would be the applicable standard of review if the transaction were (1) recommended by a disinterested and independent special committee, *and* (2) approved by stockholders in a non-waivable vote of the majority of all the minority stockholders.[38]

I reject, however, defendants' argument that the procedures used in this case warrant application of the business judgment standard of review. Although I have determined that Hammons did not stand "on both sides" of this transaction, it

---

[37] Although I have determined that the facts of this case fall outside the ambit of *Lynch*, I am also cognizant of recent suggestions of ways to "harmonize" the standards applied to transactions that differ in form but have the effect of cashing out minority stockholders. See In re Cox Commc'ns, Inc. S'holders Litig., 879 A.2d 604, 606-07, 642-48 (Del. Ch. 2005); In re Cysive, Inc. S'holders Litig., 836 A.2d 531, 549 n.23 (Del. Ch. 2003); In re Pure Res., 808 A.2d at 443-46.

[38] Of course, it is not sufficient for the special committee to merely be disinterested and independent. Rather, the committee must be given sufficient authority and opportunity to bargain on behalf of the minority stockholders, including the ability to hire independent legal and financial advisors. Moreover, neither special committee approval nor a stockholder vote would be effective if the controlling stockholder engaged in threats, coercion, or fraud. As explained below, plaintiffs contend that the price of the minority shares was depressed as a result of Hammons's improper self-dealing conduct and that as a result the special committee and the minority stockholders were coerced into accepting the Merger. If a plaintiff were able to make such a showing, even special committee approval and a majority of the minority vote would not invoke the business judgment standard of review. Similarly, a stockholder vote would not be effective for purposes of invoking the business judgment standard of review if it were based on disclosure that contained material misstatements or omissions.

is nonetheless true that Hammons and the minority stockholders were in a sense "competing" for portions of the consideration Eilian was willing to pay to acquire JQH and that Hammons, as a result of his controlling position, could effectively veto any transaction. In such a case it is paramount—indeed, necessary in order to invoke business judgment review—that there be robust procedural protections in place to ensure that the minority stockholders have sufficient bargaining power and the ability to make an informed choice of whether to accept the third-party's offer for their shares.

Here, the vote of the minority stockholders was not sufficient both because the vote could have been waived by the special committee and because the vote only required approval of a majority of the minority stockholders voting on the matter, rather than a majority of all the minority stockholders. Defendants would no doubt argue that the special committee merely had the ability to waive the vote but chose not to waive it in this case and that the Merger was in fact approved by a majority of all the minority stockholders. Importantly, however, the majority of the minority vote serves as a complement to, and a check on, the special committee. An effective special committee, unlike disaggregate stockholders who face a collective action problem, has bargaining power to extract the highest price available for the minority stockholders. The majority of the minority vote, however, provides the stockholders an important opportunity to approve or disapprove of the work of the special committee and to stop a transaction they believe is not in their best interests. Thus, to provide sufficient protection to the minority stockholders, the majority of the minority vote must be nonwaivable, even by the special committee. Moreover, requiring approval of a majority of all the minority stockholders assures that a majority of the minority stockholders truly support the transaction, and that there is not actually "passive dissent" of a majority of the minority stockholders.

To give maximum effect to these procedural protections, they must be pre-conditions to the transaction. In other words, the lack of such requirements cannot be "cured" by the fact that they would have been satisfied if they were in place. This increases the likelihood that those seeking the approval of the minority stockholders will propose a transaction that they believe will generate the support of an actual majority of the minority stockholders. Moreover, a clear explanation of the pre-conditions to the Merger is necessary to ensure that the minority stockholders are aware of the importance of their votes and their ability to block a transaction they do not believe is fair. Accordingly, entire fairness is the appropriate standard of review in this case.

C. The Entire Fairness of the Merger

The concept of entire fairness has two components: fair dealing and fair price. These prongs are not independent, and the Court does not focus on each of them individually. Rather, the Court "determines entire fairness based on all aspects of the entire transaction." Fair dealing involves "questions of when the transaction was timed, how it was initiated, structured, negotiated, disclosed to the directors, and how the approvals of the directors and the stockholders were obtained." Fair price involves questions of "the economic and financial considerations of the proposed merger, including all relevant factors: assets, market value, earnings, future prospects, and any other elements that affect the intrinsic or inherent value of a company's stock." That the special committee approval and the majority of the minority vote were not sufficient to invoke the business judgment standard of review does not necessarily mean that defendants will be unable to prevail on the issue of fair dealing.

Hammons contends that he is entitled to summary judgment even if entire fairness is the applicable standard of review. Hammons asserts that he received less than $24 per share for his Class B shares and did not receive any consideration at the expense of the minority stockholders. In support of this assertion Hammons relies on Lehman's opinion that Hammons received less than $24 per share in actual value for his Class B shares and therefore received less per share than the minority stockholders. Plaintiffs, however, attack Lehman's opinion. For example, plaintiffs criticize Lehman's decision to value the $275 million line of credit at only $20 to $30 million dollars based on the cost to Hammons of a theoretical line of credit obtained in the market, notwithstanding that such a line of credit would not, in fact, have been available to Hammons in the open market. Plaintiffs also contend that Lehman erred by failing to account for the significant tax benefits Hammons received and the other benefits Hammons received that Lehman determined "do not have a quantifiable valuation from a financial point of view." Finally, plaintiffs contend that Lehman's analysis is not determinative on the issue of fair price because it does not account for the impact of Hammons's tax and other specialized requirements on the price obtained for the minority stockholders. These factual and legal disputes regarding the persuasive value of Lehman's opinion on the issue of fair price preclude entry of summary judgment in defendants' favor on that issue.

Because entire fairness is the appropriate standard of review and because there are material factual issues as to the fairness of the price, Hammons's motion for summary judgment on that issue is denied. Similarly, the director defendants' motion for summary judgment on that issue is also denied.

Plaintiffs contend that they have established that the Merger process involved unfair dealing, thus leaving for trial only the issue of fair price. Plaintiffs also argue that the special committee was not effective because the special committee was "coerced" to accept Hammons's offer to avoid the "worse fate" of a continuing presence of minority stockholders. I am not convinced that the special committee was ineffective merely based on the fact that Hammons was able to veto any transaction. In the first instance, there is no requirement that Hammons sell his shares. Nor is there a requirement that Hammons sell his shares to any particular buyer or for any particular consideration, should he decide in the first instance to sell them. There is no requirement that Hammons agree to a transaction that would have adverse tax implications for him. If Hammons chose not to sell his shares, the minority stockholders would have remained as minority stockholders. The mere possibility that the situation would return to the status quo, something Hammons could have chosen to do by never considering selling his shares, is not, standing alone, sufficient "coercion" to render a special committee ineffective for purposes of evaluating fair dealing.

Plaintiffs also contend, however, that the price of the minority shares before the Merger was depressed as a result of Hammons's improper self-dealing transactions. Defendants contend that any "undervaluing" of the shares merely represents the lack of control premium attributable to a minority position in the Company. I am unable, on the current record, to resolve this factual dispute, and neither plaintiffs nor defendants are entitled to summary judgment on the issue of fair dealing. Plaintiffs could prevail at trial on the issue of fair dealing if they were able to establish that the price of the minority shares was depressed as a result of Hammons's improper self-dealing conduct. If the price were depressed as a result of such conduct, then the special committee and the stockholders could have been subject to improper coercion, meaning they would have been coerced into accepting any deal, whether fair or not, to avoid remaining as stockholders. This result addresses the concern that majority stockholders may have an incentive to depress the price of minority shares through improper self-dealing so they could then buy out the minority at a low price. As explained above, however, the issues of whether the price of the minority shares was depressed as a result of such conduct, and whether, as a result, the special committee or the minority stockholders were improperly coerced into accepting the Merger, must remain for trial. Accordingly, neither plaintiffs nor defendants are entitled to summary judgment on the issue of fair dealing.[48]

* * *

III.   CONCLUSION

For the foregoing reasons, defendants' motions for summary judgment are granted in part and denied in part, and plaintiffs' motion for partial summary judgment is granted in part and denied in part. Counsel shall confer and submit a form of order that implements the rulings described above.

QUESTIONS:

---

[48]   Although the procedural protections used in this case were not sufficient to invoke business judgment protection, they could have been sufficient to shift the burden of demonstrating entire fairness to plaintiffs. As explained below, some of plaintiffs' disclosure claims have survived summary judgment. Accordingly, at this stage, I cannot conclude that the majority of the minority vote shifts the burden of demonstrating entire fairness to plaintiffs. Because of the material issues of fact that remain, I also leave open the question whether the special committee's process and approval were sufficient to shift the burden of entire fairness to plaintiffs.

1. What must defendants prove in order to avoid the entire fairness test that they failed to show?

2. Why is the ability of the Special Committee to waive the requirement of a vote of a majority of the minority fatal to business judgment review where the Special Committee did not waive the requirement?

3. Why is the requirement that a majority of the voting minority shareholders approve the transaction, rather than a majority of all such shareholders, fatal to business judgment review, especially where, in fact, a majority of all minority shareholders did vote to approve the transaction?

4. In denying summary judgment to either side on the issue of fair dealing, the Chancellor stated that Plaintiffs "could prevail at trial on the issue ... if they were able to establish that the price of the minority shares was depressed as a result of Hammons' [previous] improper self-dealing conduct." How would such wrongdoing relate to the sale process, which the court concluded was not a self-dealing freezeout by Hammons?

Add on page 885, after the Note on Majority Shareholders' Duties in Short Form Mergers: In re Pure Resources, Inc Shareholders Litigation:

Glassman v. Unocal Exploration Corporation
777 A.2d 242 (Del. 2001)

BERGER, Justice.

In this appeal, we consider the fiduciary duties owed by a parent corporation to the subsidiary's minority stockholders in the context of a "short-form" merger. Specifically, we take this opportunity to reconcile a fiduciary's seemingly absolute duty to establish the entire fairness of any self-dealing transaction with the less demanding requirements of the short-form merger statute. The statute authorizes the elimination of minority stockholders by a summary process that does not involve the "fair dealing" component of entire fairness. Indeed, the statute does not contemplate any "dealing" at all. Thus, a parent corporation cannot satisfy the entire fairness standard if it follows the terms of the short-form merger statute without more.

Unocal Corporation addressed this dilemma by establishing a special negotiating committee and engaging in a process that it believed would pass muster under traditional entire fairness review. We find that such steps were unnecessary. By enacting a statute that authorizes the elimination of the minority without notice, vote, or other traditional indicia of procedural fairness, the General Assembly effectively circumscribed the parent corporation's obligations to the minority in a short-form merger. The parent corporation does not have to establish entire fairness, and, absent fraud or illegality, the only recourse for a minority stockholder who is dissatisfied with the merger consideration is appraisal.

I. Factual and Procedural Background

Unocal Corporation is an earth resources company primarily engaged in the exploration for and production of crude oil and natural gas. At the time of the merger at issue, Unocal owned approximately 96% of the stock of Unocal Exploration Corporation ("UXC"), an oil and gas company operating in and around the Gulf of Mexico. In 1991, low natural gas prices caused a drop in both companies' revenues and earnings. Unocal investigated areas of possible cost savings and decided that, by eliminating the UXC minority, it would reduce taxes and overhead expenses.

In December 1991 the boards of Unocal and UXC appointed special committees to consider a possible merger. The UXC committee consisted of three directors who, although also directors of Unocal, were not officers or employees of the parent company. The UXC committee retained financial and legal advisors and met four times before agreeing to a merger exchange ratio of .54 shares of Unocal stock for each share of UXC. Unocal and UXC announced the merger on February 24, 1992, and it was effected, pursuant to **8 Del. C. §253**, on May 2, 1992. The Notice of Merger and Prospectus stated the terms of the merger and advised the former UXC stockholders of their appraisal rights.

Plaintiffs filed this class action, on behalf of UXC's minority stockholders, on the day the merger was announced. They asserted, among other claims, that Unocal and its directors breached their fiduciary duties of entire fairness and full disclosure. The Court of Chancery conducted a two day trial and held that: (I) the Prospectus did not contain any material misstatements or omissions; (ii) the entire fairness standard does not control in a short-form merger; and (iii) plaintiffs' exclusive remedy in this case was appraisal. The decision of the Court of Chancery is affirmed.

II. Discussion

The short-form merger statute, as enacted in 1937, authorized a parent corporation to merge with its wholly-owned subsidiary by filing and recording a certificate evidencing the parent's ownership and its merger resolution. In 1957, the statute was expanded to include parent/subsidiary mergers where the parent company owns at least 90% of the stock of the subsidiary. The 1957 amendment also made it possible, for the first time and only in a short-form merger, to pay the minority cash for their shares, thereby eliminating their ownership interest in the company. In its current form, which has not changed significantly since 1957, 8 Del. C. §253 provides in relevant part:

> (a) In any case in which at least 90 percent of the outstanding shares of each class of the stock of a corporation... is owned by another

corporation..., the corporation having such stock ownership may ... merge the other corporation ... into itself... by executing, acknowledging and filing, in accordance with §103 of this title, a certificate of such ownership and merger setting forth a copy of the resolution of its board of directors to so merge and the date of the adoption; provided, however, that in case the parent corporation shall not own all the outstanding stock of ... the subsidiary corporation[ ],... the resolution ...shall state the terms and conditions of the merger, including the securities, cash, property or rights to be issued, paid delivered or granted by the surviving corporation upon surrender of each share of the subsidiary corporation....

*   *   *

(d) In the event that all of the stock of a subsidiary Delaware corporation ... is not owned by the parent corporation immediately prior to the merger, the stockholders of the subsidiary Delaware corporation party to the merger shall have appraisal rights as set forth in Section 262 of this Title.

*   *   *

The next question presented to this Court was whether any equitable relief is available to minority stockholders who object to a short-form merger. In Stauffer v. Standard Brands Incorporated,[49] minority stockholders sued to set aside the contested merger or, in the alternative, for damages. They alleged that the merger consideration was so grossly inadequate as to constitute constructive fraud and that Standard Brands breached its fiduciary duty to the minority by failing to set a fair price for their stock. The Court of Chancery held that appraisal was the stockholders' exclusive remedy, and dismissed the complaint. This Court affirmed, but explained that appraisal would not be the exclusive remedy in a short-form merger tainted by fraud or illegality:

> [T]he exception [to appraisal's exclusivity] ... refers generally to all mergers, and is nothing but a reaffirmation of the ever-present power of equity to deal with illegality or fraud. But it has no bearing here. No illegality or overreaching is shown. The dispute reduces to nothing but a difference of opinion as to value. Indeed it is difficult to imagine a case under the short merger statute in which there could be such actual fraud as would entitle a minority to set aside the merger. This is so because the very purpose of the statute is to provide the parent corporation with a means of eliminating the minority shareholder's interest in the enterprise. Thereafter the former stockholder has only a monetary claim.[50]

---

[49]   Del.Supr., 187 A.2d 78 (1962).

[50]   187 A.2d at 80

The Stauffer doctrine's viability rose and fell over the next four decades. Its holding on the exclusivity of appraisal took on added significance in 1967, when the long-form merger statute-- §251--was amended to allow cash-out mergers. In David J. Greene & Co. v. Schenley Industries, Inc.,[51] the Court of Chancery applied Stauffer to a long-form cash- out merger. Schenley recognized that the corporate fiduciaries had to establish entire fairness, but concluded that fair value was the plaintiff's only real concern and that appraisal was an adequate remedy. The court explained:

> While a court of equity should stand ready to prevent corporate fraud and any overreaching by fiduciaries of the rights of stockholders, by the same token this Court should not impede the consummation of an orderly merger under the Delaware statutes, an efficient and fair method having been furnished which permits a judicially protected withdrawal from a merger by a disgruntled stockholder.[52]

In 1977, this Court started retreating from Stauffer (and Schenley). Singer v. Magnavox Co.[53] held that a controlling stockholder breaches its fiduciary duty if it effects a cash-out merger under §251 for the sole purpose of eliminating the minority stockholders. The Singer court distinguished Stauffer as being a case where the only complaint was about the value of the converted shares. Nonetheless, the Court cautioned:

> [T]he fiduciary obligation of the majority to the minority stockholders remains and proof of a purpose, other than such freeze-out, without more, will not necessarily discharge it. In such case the Court will scrutinize the circumstances for compliance with the Sterling [v. Mayflower Hotel Corp., Del.Supr., 93 A.2d 107 (1952)] rule of "entire fairness" and, if it finds a violation thereof, will grant such relief as equity may require. Any statement in Stauffer inconsistent herewith is held inapplicable to a §251 merger.[54]

Singer's business purpose test was extended to short-form mergers two years later in Roland International Corporation v. Najjar.[55] The Roland majority wrote:

> The short form permitted by §253 does simplify the steps necessary to effect a merger, and does give a parent corporation some certainty as to result and control as to timing. But we find nothing magic about a 90%

---

[51]   Del.Ch., 281 A.2d 30 (1971).

[52]   Id. at 36. (Citations omitted.)

[53]   Del.Supr., 380 A.2d 969 (1977).

[54]   380 A.2d at 980.

[55]   Del.Supr., 407 A.2d 1032 (1979).

ownership of outstanding shares which would eliminate the fiduciary duty owed by the majority to the minority.

* * *

As to Stauffer, we agree that the purpose of §253 is to provide the parent with a means of eliminating minority shareholders in the subsidiary but, as we observed in Singer, we did "not read the decision [Stauffer] as approving a merger accomplished solely to freeze-out the minority without a valid business purpose." We held that any statement in Stauffer inconsistent with the principles restated in Singer was inapplicable to a §251 merger. Here we hold that the principles announced in Singer with respect to a §251 merger apply to a §253 merger. It follows that any statement in Stauffer inconsistent with that holding is overruled.[56]

After Roland, there was not much of Stauffer that safely could be considered good law. But that changed in 1983, in Weinberger v. UOP, Inc.,[57] when the Court dropped the business purpose test, made appraisal a more adequate remedy, and said that it was "return[ing] to the well established principles of Stauffer ... and Schenley ... mandating a stockholder's recourse to the basic remedy of an appraisal."[58] Weinberger focused on two subjects--the "unflinching" duty of entire fairness owed by self-dealing fiduciaries, and the "more liberalized appraisal" it established.

With respect to entire fairness, the Court explained that the concept includes fair dealing (how the transaction was timed, initiated, structured, negotiated, disclosed and approved) and fair price (all elements of value); and that the test for fairness is not bifurcated. On the subject of appraisal, the Court made several important statements: (i) courts may consider "proof of value by any techniques or methods which are generally considered acceptable in the financial community and otherwise admissible in court....;"[59] (ii) fair value must be based on "all relevant factors," which include not only "elements of future value ... which are known or susceptible of proof as of the date of the merger"[60] but also, when the court finds it appropriate, "damages, resulting from the taking, which the stockholders sustain as a class;"[61] and (iii) "a plaintiff's monetary remedy ordinarily

---

[56]   407 A.2d at 1036 (Citations omitted). Justice Quillen dissented, saying that the majority created "an unnecessary damage forum" for a plaintiff whose complaint demonstrated that appraisal would have been an adequate remedy. *Id.* at 1039-40.

[57]   Del.Supr., 457 A.2d 701 (1983).

[58]   Id. at 715.

[59]   Id. at 713.

[60]   Ibid.

[61]   Ibid.

should be confined to the more liberalized appraisal proceeding herein established...."[62]

By referencing both Stauffer and Schenley, one might have thought that the Weinberger court intended appraisal to be the exclusive remedy "ordinarily" in non-fraudulent mergers where "price ... [is] the preponderant consideration outweighing other features of the merger."[63] In Rabkin v. Philip A. Hunt Chemical Corp.,[64] however, the Court dispelled that view. The Rabkin plaintiffs claimed that the majority stockholder breached its fiduciary duty of fair dealing by waiting until a one year commitment to pay $25 per share had expired before effecting a cash-out merger at $20 per share. The Court of Chancery dismissed the complaint, reasoning that, under Weinberger, plaintiffs could obtain full relief for the alleged unfair dealing in an appraisal proceeding. This Court reversed, holding that the trial court read Weinberger too narrowly and that appraisal is the exclusive remedy only if stockholders' complaints are limited to "judgmental factors of valuation."[65]

Rabkin, through its interpretation of Weinberger, effectively eliminated appraisal as the exclusive remedy for any claim alleging breach of the duty of entire fairness. But Rabkin involved a long-form merger, and the Court did not discuss, in that case or any others, how its refinement of Weinberger impacted short-form mergers. Two of this Court's more recent decisions that arguably touch on the subject are Bershad v. Curtiss-Wright Corp.[66] and Kahn v. Lynch Communication Systems, Inc.,[67] both long-form merger cases. In Bershad, the Court included §253 when it identified statutory merger provisions from which fairness issues flow:

> In parent-subsidiary merger transactions the issues are those of fairness-- fair price and fair dealing. These flow from the statutory provisions permitting mergers, 8 Del. C. §§251-253 (1983), and those designed to ensure fair value by an appraisal, 8 Del. C. §262 (1983)...;"[68]

and in Lynch, the Court described entire fairness as the "exclusive" standard of review in a cash-out, parent/subsidiary merger.[69]

Mindful of this history, we must decide whether a minority stockholder may

---

[62]   Id. at 714.

[63]   Id. at 711.

[64]   Del.Supr., 498 A.2d 1099 (1985).

[65]   498 A.2d at 1108.

[66]   Del.Supr., 535 A.2d 840 (1987).

[67]   Del.Supr., 638 A.2d 1110 (1994).

[68]   535 A.2d at 845.

[69]   638 A.2d at 1117.

challenge a short-form merger by seeking equitable relief through an entire fairness claim. Under settled principles, a parent corporation and its directors undertaking a short-form merger are self-dealing fiduciaries who should be required to establish entire fairness, including fair dealing and fair price. The problem is that §253 authorizes a summary procedure that is inconsistent with any reasonable notion of fair dealing. In a short-form merger, there is no agreement of merger negotiated by two companies; there is only a unilateral act--a decision by the parent company that its 90% owned subsidiary shall no longer exist as a separate entity. The minority stockholders receive no advance notice of the merger; their directors do not consider or approve it; and there is no vote. Those who object are given the right to obtain fair value for their shares through appraisal.

The equitable claim plainly conflicts with the statute. If a corporate fiduciary follows the truncated process authorized by §253, it will not be able to establish the fair dealing prong of entire fairness. If, instead, the corporate fiduciary sets up negotiating committees, hires independent financial and legal experts, etc., then it will have lost the very benefit provided by the statute--a simple, fast and inexpensive process for accomplishing a merger. We resolve this conflict by giving effect the intent of the General Assembly.[70] In order to serve its purpose, §253 must be construed to obviate the requirement to establish entire fairness.[71]

Thus, we again return to Stauffer, and hold that, absent fraud or illegality, appraisal is the exclusive remedy available to a minority stockholder who objects to a short-form merger. In doing so, we also reaffirm Weinberger's statements about the scope of appraisal. The determination of fair value must be based on all relevant factors, including damages and elements of future value, where appropriate. So, for example, if the merger was timed to take advantage of a depressed market, or a low point in the company's cyclical earnings, or to precede an anticipated positive development, the appraised value may be adjusted to account for those factors. We recognize that these are the types of issues frequently raised in entire fairness claims, and we have held that claims for unfair dealing cannot be litigated in an appraisal.[72] But our prior holdings simply explained that equitable claims may not be engrafted onto a statutory appraisal proceeding; stockholders may not receive recessionary relief in an appraisal. Those decisions should not be read to restrict the elements of value that properly may be considered in an appraisal.

Although fiduciaries are not required to establish entire fairness in a short-form merger, the duty of full disclosure remains, in the context of this request

---

[70]   Klotz v. Warner Communications, Inc., Del.Supr., 674 A.2d 878, 879 (1995).

[71]   We do not read Lynch as holding otherwise; this issue was not before the Court in Lynch.

[72]   Alabama By-Products Corporation v. Neal, Del.Supr., 588 A.2d 255, 257 (1991).

for stockholder action.[73] Where the only choice for the minority stockholders is whether to accept the merger consideration or seek appraisal, they must be given all the factual information that is material to that decision.[74] The Court of Chancery carefully considered plaintiffs' disclosure claims and applied settled law in rejecting them. We affirm this aspect of the appeal on the basis of the trial court's decision.[75]

III. Conclusion

Based on the foregoing, we affirm the Court of Chancery and hold that plaintiffs' only remedy in connection with the short-form merger of UXC into Unocal was appraisal.

QUESTION:

1.   Does this decision encourage parent corporations to engage in tender offers to reach the 90% ownership level in order to avoid fairness challenges?

Berger v. Pubco Corporation

Delaware Supreme Court, 2009

Before STEELE, Chief Justice, HOLLAND, BERGER, JACOBS and RIDGELY, Justices, constituting the Court *en Banc*.

Upon Appeal from the Court of Chancery. REVERSED and REMANDED.

JACOBS, Justice:

The issue on this appeal is what remedy is appropriate in a "short form" merger under 8 *Del. C.* § 253, where the corporation's minority stockholders are involuntarily cashed out without being furnished the factual information material to an informed shareholder decision whether or not to seek appraisal. The Court of Chancery held that because the notice of merger did not disclose those material facts, the minority shareholders were entitled to a "quasi-appraisal" remedy, wherein those shareholders who elect appraisal must "opt in" to the proceeding and escrow a portion of the merger proceeds they received. We conclude that although the Court of Chancery correctly found that the majority stockholder had violated its

---

[73]   See: Malone v. Brincat, Del.Supr., 722 A.2d 5 (1998) (No stockholder action was requested, but Court recognized that even in such a case, directors breach duty of loyalty and good faith by knowingly disseminating false information to stockholders.)

[74]   McMullin v. Beran, Del.Supr., 765 A.2d 910 (2000).

[75]   In Re Unocal Exploration Corporation Shareholders Litigation, Del.Ch., 2001 WL 823376 (2000).

disclosure duty, the court erred as a matter of law in prescribing this specific form of remedy.

Under *Glassman v. Unocal Exploration Corporation*, the exclusive remedy for minority shareholders who challenge a short form merger is a statutory appraisal, provided that there is no fraud or illegality, and that all facts are disclosed that would enable the shareholders to decide whether to accept the merger price or seek appraisal. But where, as here, the material facts are not disclosed, the control ling stockholder forfeits the benefit of that limited review and exclusive remedy, and the minority shareholders become entitled to participate in a "quasi-appraisal" class action to recover the difference between "fair value" and the merger price without having to "opt in" to that proceeding or to escrow any merger proceeds that they received. Because the trial court declined to order that remedy, we must reverse.

FACTUAL AND PROCEDURAL BACKGROUND

The facts pivotal to this appeal, all drawn from the Court of Chancery's Opinion deciding cross motions for summary judgment, are undisputed. Pubco Corporation ("Pubco" or "the company") is a Delaware corporation whose common shares were not publicly traded. Over 90 percent of Pubco's shares were owned by defendant Robert H. Kanner, who was Pubco's president and sole director. The plaintiff, Barbara Berger, was a Pubco minority shareholder.

Sometime before October 12, 2007, Kanner decided that Pubco should "go private." As the owner of over 90% of Pubco's outstanding shares, Kanner was legally entitled to effect a "short form" merger under 8 *Del. C.* § 253. Because that short form procedure is available only to corporate controlling shareholders,[3] Kanner formed a wholly-owned shell subsidiary, Pubco Acquisition, Inc., and transferred his Pubco shares to that entity to effect the merger. In that merger per share.

Under the short form merger statute (8 *Del. C.* § 253), the only corporate action required to effect a short term merger is for the board of directors of the parent corporation to adopt a resolution approving a certificate of merger, and to furnish the minority shareholders a notice advising that the merger has occurred and that they are entitled to seek an appraisal under 8 *Del. C.* § 262. Section 253 requires that the notice include a copy of the appraisal statute, and Delaware case law requires the parent company to disclose in the notice of merger all information

---

[3]   The short form merger procedure authorized by 8 *Del. C.* § 253 is available only where "…at
least 90% of the outstanding shares of each class of the stock of a corporation…is owned by another corporation…."

material to shareholders deciding whether or not to seek appraisal.[4]

In November 2007, the plaintiff received a written notice (the "Notice") from Pubco, advising that Pubco's controlling shareholder had effected a short form merger and that the plaintiff and the other minority stockholders were being cashed out for $20 per share. The Notice explained that shareholder approval was not required for the merger to become effective, and that the minority stockholders had the right to seek an appraisal. The Notice also disclosed some information about the nature of Pubco's business, the names of its officers and directors, the number of its shares and classes of stock, a description of related business transactions, and copies of Pubco's most recent interim and annual unaudited financial statements. The Notice also disclosed that Pubco's stock, although not publicly traded, was sporadically traded over-the-counter, and that in the twenty-two months preceding the merger there were thirty open market trades that ranged in price from $12.55 to $16.00 per share, at an average price of $13.32. Finally, the Notice provided telephone, fax and e-mail contact information where shareholders could request and obtain additional information.

In its summary judgment opinion, the Court of Chancery found that except for the financial statements, the disclosures in the Notice provided no significant detail. For example, the description of the Company comprised only five sentences, one of which vaguely stated that "[t]he Company owns other income producing assets." No disclosures relating to the company's plans or prospects were made, nor was there any meaningful discussion of Pubco's actual operations or disclosure of its finances by division or line of business. Rather, the unaudited financial statements lumped all of the company's operations together. The financial statements did indicate that Pubco held a sizeable amount of cash and securities, but did not explain how those assets were, or would be, utilized. Finally, the Notice contained no disclosure of how Kanner had determined the $20 per share merger price that he unilaterally had set.

As our law required, the company attached to the Notice a copy of the appraisal statute, but the copy attached was outdated and, therefore, incorrect. The appraisal statute had been updated by changes that became effective in August 2007—two months before the Notice was sent to shareholders—but the version attached to the Notice did not reflect those changes. Pubco never sent a corrected copy of the updated appraisal statute to its former minority stockholders.

On December 14, 2007, the plaintiff initiated this lawsuit as a class action on behalf of all Pubco minority stockholders, claiming that the class is entitled to receive the difference between the $20 per share paid to each class member and the fair value of his or her shares, irrespective of whether any class member demanded

---

[4]   *Glassman*, 777 A.2d at 248. *See also McMullen v. Beran*, 765 A.2d 910, 920 (Del. 2000) (minority shareholders must be able to make an informed decision whether to accept the tender offer price or seek an appraisal of their shares.).

appraisal. Pubco and Kanner then moved to dismiss the complaint under Court of Chancery Rule 12(b)(6). The plaintiff responded to that motion, and simultaneously filed an opening brief in support of her counter-motion for summary judgment under Court of Chancery Rule 56. Thereafter, the defendants abandoned their motion to dismiss, and filed a cross-motion for summary judgment. Briefing on the cross-motions was completed on April 22, 2008, and the Court of Chancery handed down its Memorandum Opinion on May 30, 2008, granting the cross-motions in part and denying them in part. The rulings in that Opinion were embodied in a final order and judgment entered on July 18, 2008.

THE COURT OF CHANCERY OPINION

In its Opinion, the Court of Chancery addressed two issues. They were: (1) whether the Notice contained material misstatements or omissions that constituted disclosure violations, and (2) if so, what was the appropriate remedy.

The court found two separate disclosure violations. The first, which was not contested, is that the wrong version of the appraisal statute had been attached to the Notice. That violated "the Delaware appraisal statute [which] explicitly requires its inclusion in any notice of a merger giving rise to appraisal rights." The second violation, which was disputed, was that the Notice did not disclose how Kanner set the $20 per share price. The defendants argued that that nondisclosure was not material, because Kanner could have used whatever valuation methodology he desired, including even "rolling the dice." Rejecting that argument, the trial court held:

> Defendants argue that it cannot be material, because ... in a short form merger the parent has no obligation to set a fair price and, therefore, has no obligation to explain how or why the price set is fair.... Because Kanner...did not have to set a fair price and, therefore, could have used any method–no matter how absurd–to set the merger consideration[,] Defendants argue that disclosure of [Kanner's] methodology is unnecessary.

Defendants' argument entirely misses the mark, however, because the issue is not about necessity–it is about materiality. In the context of Pubco, an unregistered company that made no public filings and whose Notice was relatively terse and short on details, the method by which Kanner set the merger consideration is a fact that is substantially likely to alter the total mix of information available to the minority stockholders. Where, as here, a minority shareholder needs to decide only whether to accept the merger consideration or to seek appraisal, the question is partially one of trust: can the minority shareholder trust that the price offered is good enough, or does it likely undervalue the Company so significantly that appraisal is a worthwhile endeavor? When faced with such a question, it would be material to know that the price offered was set by arbitrarily rolling dice. In a situation like Pubco's, where so little information is available about the Company, such a disclosure would significantly change the landscape with respect to the decision of whether or not to trust the price offered by the parent. This does not mean that Kanner should have provided picayune details about the process he used to set the price; it simply means he should have disclosed in a broad sense what the process was, assuming he followed a process at all and did not simply choose a number randomly.

Having adjudicated these disclosure violations, the Court of Chancery next considered the question of remedy. The court reasoned that in a short form merger, rescissory remedies (*i.e.*, rescission or rescissory damages) are unavailable for disclosure violations, because under Section 253 a short form merger becomes effective before any disclosures to the minority stockholders are made. Instead, therefore, "minority shareholders have a statutory right to appraisal in a merger under section 253, so a proper remedy would preserve that right.... Such a remedy is a 'quasi-appraisal.'" The issue flowing from that ruling, which the parties hotly disputed, was what the content of that quasi-appraisal remedy should be. Each side advocated a different form of quasi-appraisal and relied upon one or both of two Court of Chancery decisions that involved disclosure violations in short form, cash-out mergers. The plaintiff relied upon *Nebel v. Southwest Bancorp., Inc.*,[8] a pre-*Glassman* decision. In *Nebel*, the court determined that the appropriate remedy for the adjudicated disclosure violation was that the minority shareholders should receive the difference between the merger consideration and the fair value of their shares, to be determined in a parallel appraisal proceeding in which the shareholders were not required to "opt in." The defendants advocated the quasi-appraisal remedy awarded in *Gilliland v. Motorola, Inc.*,[9] a post-*Glassman* decision where the court "attempted to mirror as best as possible the statutory appraisal remedy [,]" by requiring the minority shareholders seeking that remedy to "opt in" and to escrow a portion of the merger consideration they received.

In the instant case, the Court of Chancery concluded that the remedy should be modeled upon that previously awarded in *Gilliland*:

> The quasi-appraisal remedy fashioned in *Gilliland* attempted to mirror as best as possible the statutory appraisal remedy. Because I agree that *Nebel* does not directly address the issue of defining the contours of the quasi-appraisal remedy, and because I believe the *Gilliland* approach wisely follows the General Assembly's instructions by patterning itself after the statute, I conclude this case is governed by *Gilliland*.

The Court directed the parties to submit "an order calling for a quasi appraisal remedy based on the *Gilliland* decision," and that should require four things:

> First, Pubco must make supplemental disclosures to address the violations discussed above; namely, Pubco must disclose the method, if any, used by

---

[8]   1995 WL 405750 (Del. Ch. July 5, 1995).

[9]   873 A.2d 305 (Del. Ch. 2005).

Kanner to set the merger consideration and must include a correct and current copy of the appraisal statute. Second, the order should "require minority stockholders to make a choice to participate in the action, in order to replicate the situation they would have faced if they had received proper notice." As in *Gilliland*, these "opt-in procedures…will not be as stringent as those under the statute[, and] stockholders seeking to opt-in will need to provide only proof of beneficial ownership of the [Pubco] shares on the merger date. Third, "this quasi-appraisal action should be structured to replicate a modicum of the risk that would inhere if this were an actual appraisal action, *i.e.*, the risk that the Court will appraise [Pubco] at less than [$20] per share and the dissenting stockholders will receive less than the merger consideration…. Finally, the order should then call for a valuation of the Pubco shares as of the date of the merger using the method prescribed by the appraisal statute.

These requirements were embodied in a final order and judgment entered by the Court of Chancery on July 18, 2008, from which the plaintiff has timely appealed.

ANALYSIS

A.   *The Claims, Issues, and Standard of Review*

Because the plaintiff challenges a short form cash-out merger under Section 253, the starting point for analysis is *Glassman*, which holds that in a short-form merger there is no "entire fairness" review and that the exclusive remedy is a statutory appraisal. *Glassman* cautions, however, that those limited review and exclusive remedy protections are not absolute or unqualified. They are available only "absent fraud or illegality." Moreover, "[a]lthough fiduciaries are not required to establish entire fairness in a short-form merger, the duty of full disclosure remains…. Where the only choice for the minority stockholders is whether to accept the merger consideration or seek appraisal, they must be given all the factual information that is material to that decision."

The question not reached, and therefore not addressed, by *Glassman* is: what consequence should flow where the fiduciary fails to observe its "duty of full disclosure"? That is the only issue before us and it is one of first impression.[16]

The Court of Chancery held that where minority shareholders who are cashed out in a short form merger are deprived of information material to deciding whether or not to seek appraisal, they are entitled to a "quasi-appraisal" remedy with the following features. First, the shareholders must be furnished the material

---

[16]   The Court of Chancery expressly determined that Pubco's majority stockholder, Kanner, did not disclose those appraisal choice-related material facts to the minority shareholders. Because the defendants-appellees have not challenged that adjudicated disclosure violation on this appeal, it is established that the duty of full disclosure mandated by *Glassman* was violated, leaving for determination only the question of remedy.

information of which they were deprived. Second, the shareholders must then be afforded an opportunity to choose whether or not to participate in an action to determine the "fair value" of their shares. Third, shareholders who choose to participate must formally "opt in" to the proceeding and place into escrow a prescribed portion of the merger consideration that they received. Paraphrasing *Gilliland*, the Court of Chancery identified the purpose of the escrow requirement as to "replicate a modicum of the risk that would inhere" if the proceeding were an actual appraisal.[17]

On appeal, the plaintiff-appellant does not contest the supplemental disclosure requirement of the order awarding the quasi-appraisal remedy, only its opt in and escrow features. The appellant claims that as a matter of law, all minority shareholders should have been treated as members of a class entitled to seek the quasi-appraisal recovery, without being burdened by any precondition or requirement that they opt in or escrow any portion of the merger proceeds paid to them. That, the plaintiff contends, is the only proper application of both *Glassman* and the short form merger statute, 8 *Del. C.* § 253.

The defendants-appellees, not surprisingly, take the opposite position. They contend that the adjudicated remedy, modeled after the Court of Chancery's earlier *Gilliland* decision, is the only outcome that properly implements the policies which underlie the Delaware appraisal statute and animate the rulings in *Glassman*.

Because the Court of Chancery has broad discretion to craft an appropriate remedy for a fiduciary violation, ordinarily reviewed for abuse of discretion. Here, however, the appellant claims that the disputed remedy was erroneous as a matter of law, because the trial court erred "in formulating or applying legal principles" and in granting summary judgment to the defendants. A claim of that kind is one that we review *de novo*.

B. *Discussion*

1) The Remedial Alternatives

To repeat, the issue presented here is: in a short form merger where the exclusive remedy is an appraisal, what is the consequence of the controlling stockholder's failure to disclose the facts material to an informed shareholder decision whether or not to elect that exclusive remedy? In the abstract, four possible alternatives present themselves, of which only two are advocated by either side. The remaining two alternatives are advocated by no party. We nonetheless identify and consider them, because to do otherwise would render our analysis truncated and incomplete.

---

[17]   Chancery Opinion, at *5. The risk being referred to is that "'a stockholder who seeks appraisal must forego all of the transactional consideration and essentially place his investment in limbo until the appraisal action is resolved.' As part of this risk, a minority stockholder faces the prospect of receiving less than the merger price in the appraisal action." *Gilliland*, 873 A.2d at 312 (quoting *Turner v. Bernstein*, 776 A.2d 530, 547-48 (Del. Ch. 2000)).

The alternatives advocated by each side, respectively, are the two forms of "quasi-appraisal" remedy earlier described. The defendants argued, and the Court of Chancery agreed, that the appropriate remedy is the quasi-appraisal ordered in *Gilliland*. Under that remedial structure, fully informed minority shareholders who "opt in" and place into escrow a portion of the consideration they received may prosecute an action to recover the difference between adjudicated "fair value" and the merger consideration. The plaintiff advocated the second alternative form of "quasi-appraisal" remedy—a class action to recover the difference between "fair value" and the merger consideration, wherein the minority shareholders are automatically treated as members of the class with no obligation to opt in or to escrow any portion of the merger consideration. Under either structure, the only issue being litigated would be the appraised "fair value" of the corporation on the date of the merger, applying established corporate valuation principles.

Of the remaining two remedial alternatives (those advocated by neither side), the first would be a "replicated appraisal" proceeding that would duplicate the precise sequence of events and requirements of the appraisal statute. Under the "replicated appraisal" approach, the minority shareholders would receive (in a supplemental disclosure) all information material to making an informed decision whether to elect appraisal. Shareholders who elect appraisal would then make a formal demand for appraisal and remit to the corporation their stock certificates and the entire merger consideration that they received. Thereafter, the corporation would have the opportunity, as contemplated by the appraisal statute, to attempt to reach a settlement with the appraisal claimants. Where no settlement is reached, a formal appraisal action could then be commenced by the dissenting shareholders or by the corporation.

Under the fourth alternative (also not advocated by either side), there would be no remedial appraisal proceeding at all. Rather, the consequence of the fiduciary's adjudicated failure to disclose material facts would be to render *Glassman* inapplicable. As a result, the remedy would be the same as in a "long form" cash out merger under 8 *Del. C.* § 251—a shareholder class action for breach of fiduciary duty, where the legality of the merger (and the liability of the controlling stockholder fiduciaries) are determined under the traditional "entire fairness" review standard.

(2) Selecting The Most Appropriate Alternative

The four alternative possibilities having been identified, the question then becomes: which remedy is the most appropriate—the one ordered by the Court of Chancery or one of the three alternative forms? To decide that issue, we must first answer a predicate question: by what analytical standard do we determine which remedial alternative is optimal? We conclude that the optimal alternative would be the remedy that best effectuates the policies underlying the short form merger statute (Section 253), the appraisal statute (Section 262) and the *Glassman* decision, taking into account considerations of practicality of implementation and fairness to the litigants. A reasoned application of that standard permits the remedial alternatives to be ranked in an objective and transparent way.

Applying that standard leads us to conclude that the fourth alternative would merit the lowest priority. Under that alternative, a violation of the disclosure requirement would render *Glassman* inapplicable and deprive the majority stockholder fiduciary of the benefit of *Glassman*'s limited review and exclusive remedy. In that setting (to reiterate), the minority shareholders would be entitled to the same remedies as are available in a fiduciary duty class action challenging a long form merger.

The strongest argument favoring this approach would run as follows: under *Glassman*, full disclosure of all material facts is a necessary condition for the fiduciary to enjoy *Glassman*'s limited review and exclusive appraisal remedy. Therefore, a violation of that disclosure condition should deprive the fiduciary of those benefits. That argument, although unassailable in terms of logic and equity,[23] is flawed in one highly important respect. To accept it would disregard the intent of the General Assembly, as described in *Glassman* and *Stauffer v. Standard Brands, Incorporated*, that in a legally valid, non-fraudulent, short form merger the minority shareholders' remedy should be limited to an appraisal. Moreover, validating such an approach would disserve the purpose of *Glassman*'s disclosure requirement, which is to enable the minority stockholders to make an informed decision whether or not to seek an appraisal. A remedy that sidesteps appraisal altogether would frustrate that purpose.

Unlike this approach, the remaining three alternative remedies would give effect (albeit in varying degrees) to that legislative intent. Therefore, in the hierarchy those alternative remedies should rank above the one that abjures appraisal.

That observation brings into focus a second alternative—the "replicated appraisal" remedy that would duplicate precisely the sequence of events and requirements of the appraisal statute. Under that approach, the minority shareholders would receive a supplemental disclosure, to enable them to make an informed decision whether or not to elect an appraisal. Shareholders who elect that remedy must then make a formal demand for an appraisal, and then remit to the corporation their stock certificates and all the merger consideration they received.

This approach would place the minority shareholders in the situation they would find themselves had they received proper disclosure to begin with. The

---

[23]   More specifically, one could argue that *Glassman*'s interpretation of Section 253 (reflecting a legislative intent to limit the judicial remedy in short form mergers to a statutory appraisal) is expressly made subject to the fiduciary limitation that the majority stockholder fiduciary must disclose to the minority shareholders all material facts that would enable them to decide whether to choose that exclusive remedy. The logic of that argument would run thusly: if the fiduciary fails to do equity (by making the required disclosure), then equity will deprive the fiduciary of the benefit of the limited and exclusive judicial remedy, and subject the fiduciary to the full range of remedies otherwise available to shareholders that were cashed out in a going private merger.

strongest argument favoring this alternative is that it would give maximum effect to the legislative intent recognized in *Glassman*. The flaw of this approach, however, is that it would effectuate that legislative intent at an unacceptable cost measured in terms of practicality of application and fairness to the minority. In *Gilliland*, the Court of Chancery so recognized, implicitly acknowledging the impracticality of such an approach by refusing to order a "replicated appraisal" remedy:

> The opt-in procedures to be followed, however, will not be as stringent as those under the statute. For example, the court will not require beneficial or "street name" owners to "demand" quasi-appraisal through their record holder. The court is concerned that, given the substantial passage of time since the merger, it would be difficult for stockholders to secure the cooperation of the former record holders or nominees needed to perfect demand in accordance with the statute. Instead, stockholders seeking to opt-in will need to provide only proof of beneficial ownership of [their] shares on the merger date.

The *Gilliland* court also recognized (again, implicitly) that it would be unfair to require shareholders who desire an appraisal to remit the entire merger consideration they received *to the corporation*, as would occur in a replicated appraisal. Instead, the court required only that "those stockholders who choose to participate in the action to pay *into escrow a portion* of the merger consideration they have already received." The *Gilliland* court thereby acknowledged the unfairness of requiring the minority stockholders to bear the risk of the corporation's creditworthiness, which would result from their having to pay back a portion of the merger proceeds to the company. Instead, the court ordered that the proceeds be placed into an escrow account, with the escrowed funds representing only a portion of the merger consideration the minority actually received.

Implicit in the *Gilliland* remedy is the recognition that it is unfair to the minority shareholders, on whose behalf significant litigation expense and effort were successfully devoted, to limit their relief to requiring the fiduciary merely to fulfill the disclosure obligation it had all along. A remedy limited to awarding a second statutory appraisal would deny the minority any credit for that expense and effort, after having been forced to prosecute that litigation solely because the controlling shareholder had violated its fiduciary duty. A replicated appraisal remedy would also give controlling shareholders little incentive to observe their disclosure duty in future cases, since the cost of the remedy to the controllers would be negligible. Both in *Gilliland* and in this case the Court of Chancery eschewed that approach, concluding instead that the appropriate remedy should be a "quasi appraisal." Both parties agree with that conclusion, and so do we.

That requires us to choose between the two dueling forms of quasi-appraisal advocated by the parties on this appeal. Both forms would entitle the minority stockholders to supplemental disclosure enabling them to make an informed decision whether to participate in the lawsuit or to retain the merger proceeds. Both forms would entitle those who elect to participate to seek a recovery of the difference between the fair value of their shares and the merger consideration they received, without having to establish the controlling shareholders' personal liability for breach of fiduciary duty. The difference between the two quasi-appraisal approaches is that under the defendants' approach (which the Court of Chancery approved), the minority shareholders who elect to participate would be required to "opt in" and to escrow a prescribed portion of the merger proceeds they received. Under the plaintiff's approach, all minority stockholders would automatically become members of the class without being required to "opt in" or to escrow any portion of the merger proceeds.

As thus narrowed, the final issue may be stated as follows: under the standard we have applied, which remedy is the more appropriate—the one that imposes the opt in and partial escrow requirements or the one that does not? Considerations of utility and fairness impel us to conclude that the latter is the more appropriate remedy for the disclosure violation that occurred here. Because neither the opt-in nor the escrow requirement is mandated as a matter of law and because those requirements involve different equities,[27] we analyze each requirement separately.

We start with the "opt in" issue. The approach adopted by the Court of Chancery requires the minority shareholders to opt in to become members of the plaintiff class. The other choice would treat those shareholders automatically as members of the class—that is, as having already opted in. Those shareholders would continue as members of the class, unless and until individual members opt out after receiving the remedial supplemental disclosure and the Rule 23 notice of class action informing them of their opt out right. From the minority's standpoint, the first alternative is potentially more burdensome than the second, because shareholders that fail either to opt in or to opt in within a prescribed time, forfeit the opportunity to seek an appraisal recovery. On the other hand, structuring the remedy as an "opt out" class action avoids that risk of forfeiture, and thus benefits the

---

[27]   The Court of Chancery imposed the opt in and escrow requirements because that was the relief ordered in *Gilliland*. The *Gilliland* court imposed those requirements not because they were required as a matter of law, but because the court viewed them as an appropriate exercise of equitable discretion. Only if the *Gilliland* court had ordered a remedy taking the form of a "replicated" appraisal would strict adherence to the letter of the appraisal statute have been required. In such a case, the minority shareholders would have to opt in by making the formal demand called for by the appraisal statute, and would have to return *all* of the merger proceeds they received *to the corporation*. In *Gilliland*, however, the court required only that the shareholders remit only a portion of the merger proceeds, and then only to an escrow fund, not the corporation. Clearly, the *Gilliland* court was attempting to craft a remedy that in some aspects resembled a statutory appraisal, yet eliminated the aspects of appraisal that, in the court's view, would operate inequitably in this remedial setting. 873 A.2d at 311 ("Therefore, the court must look beyond the [appraisal] statute to fashion a proper remedy."). The critical point is that, in analyzing whether the opt in and escrow requirements imposed in *Gilliland* and this case are remedially appropriate, those requirements are not the subject of any pre-existing legal mandate.

minority shareholders. To the corporation, however, neither alternative is more burdensome than the other. Under either alternative the company will know at a relatively early stage which shareholders are (and are not) members of the class.

Given these choices, it is self evident which alternative is optimal. As between an opt in requirement that would potentially burden shareholders desiring to seek an appraisal recovery but would impose no burden on the corporation, and an opt out requirement that would impose a lesser burden on the shareholders but again no burden on the corporation, the latter alternative is superior and is the remedy that the trial court should have ordered.

That leaves the requirement that the minority shareholders electing to participate in the quasi-appraisal must escrow a portion of the merger proceeds that they received. The rationale for this requirement, as stated in *Gilliland*, is "to mimic, at least in small part, the risks of a statutory appraisal ... to promote well reasoned judgments by potential class members and to avoid awarding a 'windfall' to those shareholders who made an informed decision [after receiving the original notice of merger] to take the cash rather than pursue their statutory appraisal remedy."

The defendants-appellees argue that it is fair and equitable to require the minority shareholders to escrow some portion of the merger proceeds. Otherwise (defendants say), the shareholders would have it both ways: they could retain the merger proceeds they received and at the same time litigate to recover a higher amount—a dual benefit they would not have in an actual appraisal. It is true that the minority shareholders would enjoy that "dual benefit." But, does that make it inequitable from the fiduciary's standpoint? We think not. No positive rule of law cited to us requires replicating the burdens imposed in an actual statutory appraisal. Indeed, our law allows the minority to enjoy that dual benefit in the related setting of a class action challenging a long form merger on fiduciary duty grounds. In that setting the shareholder class members may retain the merger proceeds and simultaneously pursue the class action remedy. The defendants cite no case authority, nor are we aware of any, holding that that in the long form merger context that benefit is inequitable to the majority shareholder accused of breaching its fiduciary duty.

Lastly, fairness requires that the corporation be held to the same strict standard of compliance with the appraisal statute as the minority shareholders. Our case law is replete with examples where dissenting minority shareholders that failed to comply strictly with certain technical requirements of the appraisal statute, were held to have lost their entitlement to an appraisal, and, consequently, lost the opportunity to recover the difference between the fair value of their shares and the merger price. These technical statutory violations were not curable, so that irrespective of the equities the unsuccessful appraisal claimant could not proceed anew. That result effectively allowed the corporation to retain the entire difference between fair value and the merger price attributable to the shares for which appraisal rights were lost. The appraisal statute should be construed evenhandedly, not as a one-way street. Minority shareholders who fail to observe the appraisal statute's technical requirements risk forfeiting their statutory entitlement[30] to recover the fair value of their shares. In fairness, majority stockholders that deprive their minority shareholders of material information should forfeit their statutory right to retain the merger proceeds payable to shareholders who, if fully informed, would have elected appraisal.

In cases where the corporation does not comply with the disclosure requirement mandated by *Glassman*, the quasi-appraisal remedy that operates in the fairest and most balanced way and that best effectuates the legislative intent underlying Section 253, is the one that does not require the minority shareholders seeking a recovery of fair value to escrow a portion of the merger proceeds they received. We hold, for these reasons, that the quasi-appraisal remedy ordered by the Court of Chancery was legally erroneous in the circumstances presented here.

***

To summarize: where there is a breach of the duty of disclosure in a short form merger, the *Gilliland* approach does not appropriately balance the equities. If only a technical and non-prejudicial violation of 8 *Del. C.* § 253 had occurred, the result might be different. In some circumstances, for example, where stockholders receive an incomplete copy of the appraisal statute with their notice of merger, the *Gilliland* remedy might arguably be supportable. But the majority stockholder's duty of disclosure provides important protection for minority stockholders being cashed out in a short form merger. This protection—the quasi-appraisal remedy for a violation of that fiduciary disclosure obligation—should not be restricted by opt in or escrow requirements.

CONCLUSION

For the foregoing reasons, the judgment of the Court of Chancery is reversed, and the case is remanded for proceedings consistent with this Opinion.

---

[30] *See, e.g., Raab v. Villager Indus., Inc.*, 355 A.2d 888, 892-94 (Del. 1976) (requiring strict compliance with the "demand for payment" and "timely delivery" requirements of the appraisal statute); *Tabbi v. Pollution Control Indus., Inc.*, 508 A.2d 867, 873 (Del. Ch. 1986) (overruled on other grounds by *Enstar Corp. v. Senouf*, 535 A.2d 1351, 1357 n.7 (Del. 1987)) (persons who were not record shareholders as of the merger date, even though they filed a timely demand for appraisal, held not entitled to appraisal)); *Konfirst v. Willow CSN, Inc.*, 2006 WL 3803469, at *1 (Del. Ch. Dec. 14, 2006) (holding that appraisal demands postmarked after the statutory deadline were time-barred, despite shareholders' claim that their receipt of a notice of merger was delayed because they moved or were on vacation). Our cases hold that although the requirements of the appraisal statute are to be liberally construed for the protection of objecting stockholders, that must be done within the boundaries of orderly corporate procedures and the purpose of the requirement. *Rabb v. Villager Indus., Inc.*, 355 A.2d at 891 (citing *Salt Dome Oil Corp. v. Schenck*, 41 A.2d 583 (Del. Ch. 1945); and *Carl M. Loeb Rhoades & Co. v. Hilton Hotels Corp.*, 222 A.2d 789 (Del. 1986)).

Questions

1.   The only violation of the disclosure requirements found by the Court of Chancery was a failure to disclose the manner in which the controlling shareholder set the merger price. The disclosures contained only historical financial information, without any projections or detailed descriptions of all of the corporation's businesses and properties. What are the implications for the disagreement between Chancellor Strine (Pure Resources; Netsmart) and other members of the Chancery Court over the need to disclose any existing projections (Skeen v. Jo Ann Stores)?

2.   If you were the lawyer who failed to attach the correct current copy of the statute to the notice to minority shareholders, what do you say to your client after this decision? The opinion states that "Section 253 requires that the notice include a copy of the appraisal statute. . . ." Can you locate that requirement?

3.   If this is an equitable action, why does Weinberger's entire fairness standard not apply?

Add on page 890, after QUESTIONS

6.   Appraisal Exceptions and Form Over Substance

Louisiana Mun. Police Employees' Retirement System v. Crawford

918 A.2D 1172 (Del. Ch. 2007)

Chandler, Chancellor.

[Caremark was concerned that it was an intermediary between pharmaceutical companies and health plans, and that this could cause it to be eliminated as a cost-cutting move. Caremark had discussions with two companies about business combinations – Express Scripts, another intermediary, where negotiations terminated after a disappointing earnings report by Express Scripts – and CVS. The Caremark - CVS combination was always envisioned as a stock-for-stock "merger of equals" where neither side would be seen as the acquiror, and both companies would have equal board representation. When an agreement was reached, it was agreed that Caremark stockholders would own about 45% of the combined company, in a stock-for-stock merger. The agreement contained a "force the vote" provision similar to that in the Omnicare case, a no-shop provision and a "last look" provision that gave either party a right of first refusal if a better offer were received. Each party committed to a termination fee of $675 million if either board changed its recommendation of the merger and the company merged with another suitor within twelve months.

This agreement, approved by both boards on November 1, 2006, was disrupted by Express Script's higher bid for Caremark on December 15. The bid was 15% higher than the closing price of Caremark stock at the time, or over $3 billion more than the value of the CVS deal. Thereafter Ryan, CEO of CVS, called Crawford, CEO of Caremark, and proposed that Caremark declare a special dividend at the time of the merger, to enhance the merger consideration for Caremark shareholders. The dividend would be declared before the merger, but would be payable only if the Caremark shareholders approved the merger.

Express Scripts sued to enjoin the merger on various grounds, but the most innovative one involved the claim that the Caremark proxy statement failed to inform its shareholders that they had appraisal rights under Del. GCL §262. This section provides that appraisal is not available for shareholders of a public company who receive shares in another public company.]

VI. APPRAISAL RIGHTS

Plaintiffs contend the $6 special cash dividend triggers appraisal rights under 8 *Del. C.* §262. Defendants respond that the special dividend has been approved and will be payable by Caremark and, thus, has independent legal significance preventing it from being recognized as merger consideration. Thus, according to defendants, dissenting Caremark shareholders will have no appraisal rights after the CVS/Caremark merger.

Section 262 of the DGCL grants appraisal rights to stockholders who are required, by the terms of the merger, to accept any consideration other than shares of stock in the surviving company, shares of stock listed on a national securities exchange, or cash received as payment for fractional shares. The $6 "special dividend," although issued by the Caremark board, is fundamentally cash consideration paid to Caremark shareholders on behalf of CVS.

Defendants are unsuccessful in their efforts to cloak this cash payment as a "special dividend." CVS and Caremark filed a joint proxy in which they informed shareholders of the merger terms and recommended merger approval. This proxy statement lists details of the special cash dividend:

> CVS separately granted a waiver to Caremark from the restrictions set forth in Section 6.01(b) of the merger agreement to permit Caremark to pay a one-time, special cash dividend to holders of record of Caremark common stock (on a record date to be set by the Caremark board of directors) in the amount of $2.00 per share of Caremark common stock held by each such holder on such record date, which dividend shall, under the terms of the CVS waiver, be declared prior to the Caremark special meeting, but *shall only become payable upon or after the effective time of the merger, and such payment shall be conditioned upon occurrence of the effective time of the merger.*

Thus, defendants specifically condition payment of the $6 cash "special dividend" on shareholder approval of the merger agreement. Additionally, the payment becomes due upon or even **after** the effective time of the merger. These facts belie the claim that the special dividend has legal significance independent of the merger. CVS, by terms of the CVS/Caremark merger agreement, controls the value of the dividend. Defendants even warn in their public disclosures that the special cash dividend might be treated as merger consideration for tax purposes. In this case, the label "special dividend" is simply cash consideration dressed up in a →H none-too-convincing disguise. When merger consideration includes partial cash and stock payments, shareholders are entitled to appraisal rights. So long as payment of the special dividend remains conditioned upon shareholder approval of the merger, Caremark shareholders should not be denied their appraisal rights simply because their directors are willing to collude with a favored bidder to "launder" a cash payment. As Caremark failed to inform shareholders of their appraisal rights, the meeting must be enjoined for at least the statutorily required notice period of twenty days.

* * *

VIII. CONCLUSION

Based on the foregoing reasons, this Court enjoins any vote of Caremark shareholders with respect to the CVS/Caremark merger for at least twenty days after defendants properly disclose to shareholders (a) their right to seek appraisal and (b) the structure of fees paid to Caremark's bankers. At this stage, however, no broader injunction is necessary. The balance of the equities weighs in favor of permitting informed shareholders to speak directly to their fiduciaries without further intervention by this Court.

No party should infer from the fact that I am denying plaintiffs an injunction that existence of appraisal rights and the disclosure of all material information to informed, disinterested shareholders somehow excuses violations of fiduciary duties under Delaware law. This Opinion addresses only a preliminary injunction, an extraordinary remedy granted to parties in order to preserve rights that would otherwise be extinguished over the course of litigation. * * *

QUESTIONS

1. The court characterizes Caremark's cash dividend to its own shareholders as "fundamentally paid to Caremark shareholders on behalf of CVS." What reasoning underlies this conclusion?

2. Recall the discussion of "independent legal significance" following Hariton v. Arco Electronics, Inc. in Chapter Four, Part 4.A, at pages 122-26. Recall that while Keller v. Wilson held that unpaid preferred dividends were vested property rights that could not be divested by a charter amendment, Federal United Corp. v. Havender held that a merger was an act of independent legal significance, and that preferred share rights could be altered in that way. What effect does this decision have on your confidence

that those decisions will be followed in the future?

Add after iii.   WHAT IS "BENEFICIAL OWNERSHIP?" on page 949:

CSX Corporation v. The Children's Investment Fund

562 F. Supp. 2d 511 (S.D. N.Y. 2008)

Lewis A. Kaplan, United States District Judge.

Some people deliberately go close to the line dividing legal from illegal if they see a sufficient opportunity for profit in doing so. A few cross that line and, if caught, seek to justify their actions on the basis of formalistic arguments even when it is apparent that they have defeated the purpose of the law.

This is such a case. The defendants -- two hedge funds that seek extraordinary gain, sometimes through "shareholder activism" -- amassed a large economic position in CSX Corporation ("CSX"), one of the nation's largest railroads. They did so for the purpose of causing CSX to behave in a manner that they hoped would lead to a rise in the value of their holdings. And there is nothing wrong with that. But they did so in close coordination with each other and without making the public disclosure required of 5 percent shareholders and groups by the Williams Act, a statute that was enacted to ensure that other shareholders are informed of such accumulations and arrangements. They now have launched a proxy fight that, if successful, would result in their having substantial influence and perhaps practical working control of CSX.

Defendants seek to defend their secret accumulation of interests in CSX by invoking what they assert is the letter of the law. Much of their position in CSX was in the form of total return equity swaps ("TRSs"), a type of derivative that gave defendants substantially all of the indicia of stock ownership save the formal legal right to vote the shares. In consequence, they argue, they did not beneficially own the shares referenced by the swaps and thus were not obliged to disclose sooner or more fully than they did. In a like vein, they contend that they did not reach a formal agreement to act together, and therefore did not become a "group" required to disclose its collaborative activities, until December 2007 despite the fact that they began acting in concert with respect to CSX far earlier. But these contentions are not sufficient to justify defendants' actions.

The question whether the holder of a cash-settled equity TRS beneficially owns the referenced stock held by the short counterparty appears to be one of first impression. There are persuasive arguments for concluding, on the facts of this case, that the answer is "yes" -- that defendants beneficially owned at least some and quite possibly all of the referenced CSX shares held by their counterparties. But it ultimately is unnecessary to reach such a conclusion to decide this case.

Rule 13d-3(b) under the Exchange Act [1] provides in substance that one who creates an arrangement that prevents the vesting of beneficial ownership as part of a plan or scheme to avoid the disclosure that would have been required if the actor bought the stock outright is deemed to be a beneficial owner of those shares. That is exactly what the defendants did here in amassing their swap positions. In consequence, defendants are deemed to be the beneficial owners of the referenced shares.

As for the question whether defendants made prompt disclosure after they formed a "group" within the meaning of Section 13(d) of the Exchange Act, the evidence, as in virtually all such cases, is circumstantial. But it quite persuasively demonstrates that they formed a group many months before they filed the necessary disclosure statement. Their protestations to the contrary rest in no small measure on the premise that they avoided forming a group by starting conversations by stating that they were not forming a group and by avoiding entry into a written agreement. But the Exchange Act is concerned with substance, not incantations and formalities.

This is not to say that CSX is entitled to all of the relief that it seeks. The Williams Act was intended not only to prevent secret accumulation and undisclosed group activities with respect to the stock of public companies, but to do so without "tipping the balance of regulation either in favor of management or in favor of the person making the takeover bid."[2] It must be applied, especially in private litigation, with due regard for the principle that the purpose of private equitable relief is "to deter, not to punish."[3] Moreover, the Court's ability to formulate a remedy is sharply constrained by precedent. Accordingly, while the Court will enjoin defendants from further Section 13(d) violations, it may not preclude defendants from voting their CSX shares and declines to grant any of the other drastic relief that CSX seeks. Any penalties for defendants' violations must come by way of appropriate action by the Securities and Exchange Commission ("SEC") or the Department of Justice.

I.   Parties

Plaintiff CSX Corporation ("CSX") is incorporated in Virginia and headquartered in Jacksonville, Florida. Its shares are traded on the New York Stock Exchange, and it operates one of the nation's largest rail systems through its wholly owned subsidiary, CSX Transportation, Inc. Its chairman, president, and chief executive officer is Michael J. Ward, who is named here as an additional defendant on the counterclaims.

Defendants The Children's Investment Fund Management (UK) LLP ("TCIF UK")[4] and The Children's Investment Fund Management (Cayman) LTD. ("TCIF Cayman") are, respectively, an English limited liability partnership and a Cayman Islands company. Defendant The Children's Investment Master Fund ("TCI Fund") also is a company organized under the laws of the Cayman Islands and is managed by both TCIF UK and TCIF Cayman. These entities are run by defendant Christopher Holm, who is managing partner and a controlling person of TCIF UK and the sole owner and a controlling person of TCIF Cayman. Defendant Snehal

Amin is a partner of TCIF UK. These five defendants are referred to collectively as TCI.

Defendants 3G Fund L.P. ("3G Fund") and 3G Capital Partners L.P. ("3G LP") are Cayman Islands limited partnerships. Defendant 3G Capital Partners Ltd. ("3G Ltd.") is a Cayman Islands company and the general partner of 3G LP, which in turn is the general partner of 3G Fund. They are run by defendant Alexandre Behring, also known as Alexandre Behring Costa, who is the managing partner of 3G Ltd. These four defendants are referred to collectively as 3G.

II.   Proceedings

TCI and 3G currently are engaged in a proxy fight in which they seek, *inter alia,* to elect their nominees to five of the twelve seats on the CSX board of directors and to amend its by-laws to permit holders of 15 percent of CSX shares to call a special meeting of shareholders at any time for any purpose permissible under Virginia law. The CSX annual meeting of shareholders, which is the object of the proxy fight, is scheduled to take place on June 25, 2008.

CSX brought this action against TCI and 3G on March 17, 2008. The complaint alleges, among other things, that defendants failed timely to file a Schedule 13D after forming a group to act with reference to the shares of CSX and that both the Schedule 13D and the proxy statement they eventually filed were false and misleading. [4] It seeks, among other things, an order requiring corrective disclosure, voiding proxies defendants have obtained, and precluding defendants from voting their CSX shares. TCI Master Fund, 3G Fund, 3G LP, and 3G Ltd. filed counterclaims against CSX and Ward asserting various claims under the federal securities laws. [5]

*   *   *

III.   Total Return Swaps

A.   The Basics

The term "derivative," as the term is used in today's financial world, refers to a financial instrument that derives its value from the price of an underlying instrument or index. Among the different types of derivatives are swaps, instruments whereby two counterparties agree to "exchange cash flows on two financial instruments over a specific period of time." These are (1) a "reference obligation" or "underlying asset" such as a security, a bank loan, or an index, and (2) a benchmark loan, generally with an interest rate set relative to a commonly used reference rate (the "reference rate") such as the London Inter-Bank Offered Rate ("LIBOR"). A TRS is a particular form of swap.

The typical–or "plain vanilla"–TRS is represented by Figure 1.

Figure 1

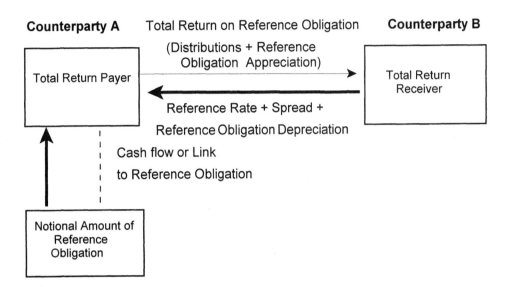

Counterparty A -- the "short" party -- agrees to pay Counterparty B -- the "long" party -- cash flows based on the performance of a defined underlying asset in exchange for payments by the long party based on the interest that accrues at a negotiated rate on an agreed principal amount (the "notional amount"). More specifically, Counterparty B, which may be referred to as the "total return receiver" or "guarantor," is entitled to receive from Counterparty A the sum of (1) any cash distributions, such as interest or dividends, that it would have received had it held the referenced asset, and (2) either (i) an amount equal to the market appreciation in the value of the referenced asset over the term of the swap (if the TRS is cash-settled) or, what is economically the same thing, (ii) the referenced asset in exchange for its value on the last refixing date prior to the winding up of the transaction (if the TRS is settled in kind). Counterparty A, referred to as the "total return payer" or "beneficiary," is entitled to receive from Counterparty B (1) an amount equal to the interest at the negotiated rate that would have been payable had it actually loaned Counterparty A the notional amount, [13] and (2) any decrease in the

---

[13]   The notional amount typically is the value of the referenced asset at the time the transaction is agreed and may be recalculated periodically. Subrahmanyam Report P 63 . The difference between the reference rate and the negotiated interest rate of the swap depends on (1) the creditworthiness of the two parties, (2) characteristics of the underlying asset, (3) the total return payer's cost of financing, risk, and desired profit, and (4) market competition. *Id.* P 64.

market value of the referenced asset. [14]

For example, in a cash-settled TRS with reference to 100,000 shares of the stock of General Motors, the short party agrees to pay to the long party an amount equal to the sum of (1) any dividends and cash flow, and (2) any increase in the market value that the long party would have realized had it owned 100,000 shares of General Motors. The long party in turn agrees to pay to the short party the sum of (1) the amount equal to interest that would have been payable had it borrowed the notional amount from the short party, and (2) any depreciation in the market value that it would have suffered had it owned 100,000 shares of General Motors.

In practical economic terms, a TRS referenced to stock places the long party in substantially the same economic position that it would occupy if it owned the referenced stock or security. There are two notable exceptions. First, since it does not have record ownership of the referenced shares, it does not have the right to vote them. Second, the long party looks to the short party, rather than to the issuer of the referenced security for distributions and the marketplace for any appreciation in value.

The short party of course is in a different situation. It is entitled to have the long party place it in the same economic position it would have occupied had it advanced the long party an amount equal to the market value of the referenced security. But there are at least two salient distinctions, from the short party's perspective, between a TRS and a loan. First, the short party does not actually advance the notional amount to the long party. Second, it is subject to the risk that the referenced asset will appreciate during the term of the TRS. As will appear, the institutions that make a business of serving as short parties in TRSs deal with this exposure by hedging, a fact pivotal to one of CSX's claims here.

The swap agreements at issue in this case are cash-settled TRSs entered into by TCI with each of eight counterparties, most significantly Deutsche Bank AG ("Deutsche Bank") and Citigroup Global Markets Limited ("Citigroup"), and by 3G with Morgan Stanley.

B.   The Purposes of TRSs

The goals of those who enter into TRSs vary.

1.   Short Parties

As a generic matter, a short party may be motivated to enter into a TRS simply to obtain the cash flow generated by the long party's payment of the negotiated rate on the notional amount over the term of the swap. But the *quid pro quo* for that cash flow is the exposure to the risk of market appreciation in the referenced security.

As a matter of theory and on occasion in practice, a short party may accept that exposure either because it thinks the risk of appreciation is small -- in other words, it is making its own investment decision with respect to the referenced security -- or because it has a more or less offsetting long exposure that it wishes to hedge. But that is not what we are dealing with in this case.

The defendants' counterparties in this case are major financial service institutions that are in the business, among others, of offering TRSs as a product or service and seeking an economic return via the pseudo-interest, if it may be so called, that they receive on the notional amount and from other incidental revenue sources. They are not, in this aspect of their endeavors, in the business of speculating on the market fluctuation of the shares referenced by the TRSs into which they enter as short parties. Accordingly, they typically hedge their short exposures by purchasing the referenced securities in amounts identical to those referenced in their swap agreements.

Institutions that hedge short TRS exposure by purchasing the referenced shares typically have no economic interest in the securities. They are, however, beneficial owners and thus have the right to vote the referenced shares.[18]

Institutional voting practices appear to vary. As noted below, some take the position that they will not vote shares held to hedge TRS risk. Some may be influenced, at least in some cases, to vote as a counterparty desires. Some say they vote as they determine in their sole discretion. Of course, one may suppose that banks seeking to attract swap business well understand that activist investors will consider them to be more attractive counterparties if they vote in favor of the positions their clients advocate. In any case, however, the accumulation of substantial hedge positions significantly alters the corporate electorate. It does so by (1) eliminating the shares constituting the hedge positions from the universe of available votes, (2) subjecting the voting of the shares to the control or influence of a long party that does not own the shares, or (3) leaving the vote to be determined by an institution that has no economic interest in the fortunes of the issuer, holds nothing more than a formal interest, but is aware that future swap business from a particular client may depend upon voting in the "right" way.

2. Long Parties

A long party to a TRS referencing equity in a public company gains economic exposure to the equity. In other words, it is exposed to essentially the same potential benefits and detriments as would be the case if it held the referenced security, and it gains that exposure without the need for the capital to fund or maintain such a purchase directly. This may permit such investors to operate with greater leverage or a lower cost than might be the case if they bought the security directly. But those are by no means the only reasons motivating long parties to engage in TRSs. There can be tax advantages. Most importantly for purposes of this case, if the long party to a cash-settled TRS is not the beneficial owner of the referenced shares -- a question hotly contested here -- one interested in amassing a large economic exposure to the equity of a registered company may do so without

---

[18] This decoupling of the economic and voting interests is discussed, among other places, in Henry Hu & Bernard Black, *The New Vote Buying: Empty Voting and Hidden (Morphable) Ownership,* 79 S. CAL. L. REV. 811 (2006).

making the public disclosure that is required when a person or group acquires 5 percent or more of the outstanding shares.

The avoidance of public disclosure can confer significant advantages on the long party. By concealing its activities, it may avoid other investors bidding up the referenced stock in anticipation of a tender offer or other corporate control contest and thus maximize the long party's profit potential. Second, it permits a long party who is interested in persuading an issuer to alter its policies, but desirous of avoiding an all-out battle for control, to select the time of its emergence to the issuer as a powerful player to a moment of its choosing, which may be when its exposure is substantially greater than 5 percent. In other words, it permits a long party to ambush an issuer with a holding far greater than 5 percent.

One other point bears mention here. TRSs, like all or most derivatives, are privately negotiated contracts traded over the counter. Their terms may be varied during their lives as long as the counterparties agree. In consequence, a TRS that in its inception contemplates cash settlement may be settled in kind -- i.e., by delivery of the referenced shares to the long party -- as long as the parties consent.

This confers another potential advantage on a long party that contemplates a tender offer, proxy fight, or other corporate control contest. By entering into cash-settled TRSs, such an investor may concentrate large quantities of an issuer's stock in the hands of its short counterparties and, when it judges the time to be right, unwind those swaps by acquiring the referenced shares from those counterparties in swiftly consummated private transactions. Moreover, even if such TRSs were settled in cash, the disposition by the short counterparties of the referenced shares held to hedge their swap exposures would afford a ready supply of shares to the market at times and in circumstances effectively chosen and known principally by the long party. The long party therefore likely would have a real advantage in converting its exposure from swaps to physical shares even if it does not unwind the swaps in kind.

IV.   *The Events of Mid-2006 Until Late 2007*

The events preceding this lawsuit are best understood by first considering the conduct of TCI and 3G separately. The Court then will analyze the relationship between TCI and 3G and their conduct in order to determine whether they in fact acted independently.

A.   *TCI*

1.   *TCI Develops a Position in CSX*

TCI began to research the United States railroad industry in the second half of 2006 and rapidly focused on Norfolk Southern and CSX, the two largest railroads in the eastern portion of the country. It decided to concentrate on CSX because it "had more legacy contracts that were below market value prices" and, in TCI's view, "ran less efficiently" than did Norfolk. In short, it felt that changes in policy and, if need be, management could bring better performance and thus a higher stock price. That insight, if insight it was, however, would be worthless or, at any rate, less valuable if CSX did not act as TCI thought appropriate. So TCI embarked on a course designed from the outset to bring about changes at CSX.

TCI made its initial investment in CSX on October 20, 2006, by entering into TRSs referencing 1.4 million shares of CSX stock. By the end of that month, it was party to TRSs referencing 1.7 percent of CSX shares.

TCI almost immediately contacted CSX and informed it that TCI had accumulated approximately $100 million of CSX stock. Two weeks later, it advised CSX that it had $300 million invested in CSX, "with the potential to scale that further," and sought a meeting with senior management at the Citigroup Transportation Conference, which was scheduled to take place on November 14, 2006.

In the meantime, TCI continued accumulating TRSs referencing CSX throughout November, engaging in seventeen swap transactions with various financial institution counterparties. By the middle of the month, it had increased its exposure to approximately 2.7 percent.

On November 14, 2006, TCI's Hohn and Amin attended the Citigroup conference. During the course of the day, they approached CSX representatives, including David Baggs, the assistant vice president of treasury and investor relations. Amin later told Baggs that TCI's swaps, the only type of investment exposure TCI then had in CSX, could be converted into direct ownership at any time.

Following the conference, TCI continued to build its position through additional swaps throughout December, reaching 8.8 percent by the end of 2006.

2.   *TCI's Leveraged Buyout Proposal*

TCI's belief that it could profit substantially if it could alter CSX's policies or, if need be, management manifested itself when, during December 2006, it began to investigate the possibility of a leveraged buyout ("LBO"). It explored this possibility with Goldman Sachs, sending its LBO model. [26] Its email "re-iterate[d]" the need to keep the communication highly confidential, as TCI "ha[d] not taken the idea to anyone else, nor [was its] holding publicly disclosed so any leakage of our conversations with you would be damaging for our relations with the company."

On January 22, 2007, by which date TCI had amassed TRSs referencing 10.5 percent of CSX, TCI met with one of CSX's financial advisors, Morgan Stanley, to discuss the LBO proposal. It noted during its presentation that a "'perfect storm' of conditions makes a private equity bid [for a major U.S. railroad] nearly inevitable" and that "CSX [was] logically the prime candidate" because of its "valuation, size, [and] quality of franchise." TCI urged Morgan Stanley to back the plan and suggested that CSX "formally hire an investment bank to proceed urgently."

Morgan Stanley relayed the substance of its conversation to CSX. TCI then approached CSX directly about the issue on February 8 at an investor conference organized by J.P. Morgan. Amin asked Baggs for CSX's views on the LBO proposal. Baggs confirmed that Morgan Stanley had relayed the proposal but said that CSX was not in a position to respond.

3.   *January through March 2007*

TCI continued to build its TRS position in CSX. In the meantime, CSX was not idle. On February 14, 2007, it filed a Report of Form 8-K in which it announced a plan to buy back $ 2 billion worth of its common stock.

By February 15, 2007, the date of the BB&T Transportation Conference, which was attended by CSX, TCI, and others, TCI had increased its position, still entirely via TRSs, to 13.6 percent. At the conference, Amin approached Baggs and Oscar Munoz, CSX's chief financial officer, to inquire as to how CSX intended to conduct its share repurchase program. Baggs and Munoz declined to discuss the specifics in light of Regulation FD under the securities laws.[35] During the course of the brief conversation, however, Amin stated that TCI "owned" 14 percent of CSX.

Following the BB&T Transportation Conference, TCI began to contact other hedge funds about CSX. Hohn told Mala Gaonkar, a partner of Lone Pine Capital, to "[t]ake a look" at CSX and Vinit Bodas, managing director of Deccan Value Advisors, that "csx is the best to us keep this confidential [*sic*]." On March 2, 2007, Hohn told Bodas to "[b]uy csx [*sic*]."

These contacts, the Court finds, were intended to promote the acquisition of CSX shares by hedge funds that TCI regarded as favorably disposed to TCI and its approach to CSX in an effort to build support for whatever course of action it ultimately might choose with respect to the company. Moreover, the evidence convinces the Court that it is likely that TCI made similar approaches to other such funds. Hohn contended in his witness statement that he had conversations with hedge funds such as Deccan Value Advisors, Lone Pine Capital, 3G, Seneca, Icahn, TWC, and Atticus, but only concerning the railroad industry generally, not CSX in particular. Given the evidence to the contrary regarding Hohn's discussions with Deccan Value and Lone Pine, the Court's assessment of Hohn's credibility, and TCI's clear interest in doing so, the Court finds that Hohn did not limit his conversations with other hedge funds to industry-level topics. He suggested, in one way or another, that they buy CSX shares and alerted them to the fact that CSX had become a TCI target.

Up to this point, TCI had not acquired directly even a single share of CSX stock. But it decided to begin such acquisitions to place more pressure on the company and to lay the groundwork for a proxy fight.

---

[35]   17 C.F.R. § 243.100 *et seq.* "In general terms, Regulation FD prohibits a company and its senior officials from privately disclosing any material nonpublic information regarding the company or its securities to certain persons such as analysts or institutional investors." *SEC v. Siebel Sys., Inc.,* 384 F. Supp. 2d 694, 696 (S.D.N.Y. 2005). If the company makes selective disclosure of material nonpublic information, it must disclose the same information publicly.

On March 2, 2007, TCI filed a premerger notification report under the Hart-Scott-Rodino Antitrust Improvements Act of 1976 ("HSR Act")[41] in which it stated that it intended to acquire an undetermined number of CSX common shares in an amount that would meet or exceed $ 500 million. A few days later, Amin advised CSX of the filing by letter.

* * *

4.   *TCI Begins Preparing for a Proxy Fight*

In early April, TCI sent its LBO model to Evercore, another CSX advisor, and reached out to Hunter Harrison, the chief executive officer of Canadian National, a Class I railroad like CSX, to inquire whether "he would be interested in coming in as CEO of CSX."[49] By the middle of the month, Amin wrote that TCI was not "going to get what we want passively." At more or less the same time, TCI began to unwind some of its swaps and to purchase CSX stock with a goal of keeping its exposure to CSX "roughly constant."[51] It is relevant to consider why TCI decided to shift some of its position into shares.

Certainly there is no persuasive evidence that any economic factor that led TCI to choose swaps in the first place had changed. In other words, if financing considerations made swaps more attractive at the outset, that advantage persisted. So the explanation lies elsewhere. And it is, in the circumstances, obvious. TCI saw the payoff on its CSX investment, if there was to be one, resulting from a change in CSX policies and, if need be, management. But CSX had rebuffed all of TCI's overtures for substantive high level meetings and shown little interest in an LBO. So TCI by this time understood that a proxy fight likely would be required to gain control of or substantial influence over CSX. Holding shares that it could vote directly had an advantage over swaps because the votes of shares held by swap counterparties were less certain. They depended upon TCI's ability to influence those counterparties to vote the shares as TCI wished. This advantage, however, was not enough to cause TCI to dump a large part of its TRS position.

* * *

7.   *TCI Concentrates its Swaps in Deutsche Bank and Citigroup*

As the likelihood of a proxy fight increased, TCI began to address the matter of its voting power.

---

[49]   PX 36; PX 75. Amin explained at trial that TCI sought only to determine whether Harrison was interested, but that it was not TCI's intention "to necessarily have him as CEO of CSX." Tr. (Amin) at 200. Assuming (but not finding) that to be so, the incident nevertheless would confirm the Court's view that TCI was determined to force changes in CSX's policies and, if need be, to bring about a change in control.

[51]   DX 145 (Amin) P 37. By April 18, its combined economic exposure to CSX common, including both its directly owned shares and its swap position, reached 15.1 percent. Subrahmanyam Report Ex. C.1.

From the inception of its TRS acquisitions in October 2006 until the end of October 2007, TCI carefully distributed its swaps among eight counterparties so as to prevent any one of them from acquiring greater than 5 percent of CSX's shares and thus having to disclose its swap agreements with TCI. On October 30, 2007, however, TCI began unwinding its TRSs with Credit Suisse, Goldman Sachs, J.P. Morgan, Merrill Lynch, Morgan Stanley, and UBS and replacing them with TRSs with Deutsche Bank and Citigroup. Ultimately, it shifted exposure equal to approximately 9 percent of CSX from other counterparties into Deutsche Bank and Citigroup.

TCI contends that it did this for two reasons. It claims first that it was motivated by the credit market crisis, believing that Deutsche Bank and Citigroup, as commercial banks backed by governmental central banks, would reduce TCI's exposure to counterparty credit risk. Perhaps so. But there was another and, from TCI's point of view, far more important reason for this move. The likelihood of its counterparties voting the hedge shares with TCI was very much on its mind. Indeed, Hohn stated that he and Amin

> "discussed whether picking Deutsche Bank and Citigroup would be beneficial in terms of a potential vote of any hedge shares in a potential proxy fight. With respect to Deutsche Bank, we speculated that it might be helpful that a hedge fund within Deutsche Bank, Austin Friars Capital, also had a proprietary position in CSX."

But Hohn was modest. As the record demonstrates, TCI and Austin Friars had been working together, at least to some degree, on the CSX project for some time. TCI had consulted Deutsche Bank about its LBO proposal. And, as we shall see, there is additional reason to believe that Deutsche Bank was exceptionally receptive, to say the least, to TCI's goals and methods.

8.   TCI Enters into Agreements with Two Director-Nominees

TCI had met with Tim O'Toole in October to gauge his interest in being nominated for the CSX board. On December 6, 2007, O'Toole purchased 2,500 shares of CSX stock, which qualified him for election, and on December 10 entered into a formal agreement to be a nominee for the board. The next day, and after a two week negotiation, Gary Wilson also agreed to be a nominee for TCI's slate of directors.

B.   3G

1.   3G Develops a Position in CSX

3G began to analyze the investment potential of the North American railroad industry during 2005 and 2006 but began to focus on CSX only toward the end of 2006 and beginning of 2007. It claims that it perceived CSX to be 3G's best investment opportunity because it thought that (1) the share price of CSX was "less likely to decrease and more likely to appreciate over time as compared with other railroads," (2) "CSX had a large proportion of legacy contracts at below-market prices that would expire and could then be re-priced over time" to increase revenues, and (3) "CSX had substantial upside potential from improving operational efficiency."

During the first week of February, Daniel Schwartz of 3G contacted CSX's investor relations department to inquire about the company. He then emailed Behring on February 7 to indicate that the deadline had passed for CSX shareholders to submit proposals to be included in the company's proxy materials, including board nominations, for that year's annual general meeting. As 3G was not then a shareholder of CSX - indeed, it had no investments in or exposure to it of any kind -- this demonstrates its interest in a proxy fight right from the outset.

Its denial of this at trial was not credible.

* * *

VI. *The Positions of the Parties*

CSX contends that (1) TCI violated Section 13(d) of the Exchange Act by failing to disclose its beneficial ownership of shares of CSX common stock referenced in their TRSs and (2) TCI and 3G violated Section 13(d) by failing timely to disclose the formation of a group. It argues further that TCI and 3G violated Section 14(a) of the Exchange Act because their proxy statements were materially false and misleading. Its state law claim contends that defendants' notice of intent to nominate directors failed to comply with CSX's bylaws in violation of Section 13.1-624 of the Virginia Stock Corporation Act.

Defendants contend first that CSX and Ward violated Section 14(a) of the Exchange Act because the CSX proxy statement is materially false and misleading concerning (1) executive compensation and director stock awards, and (2) the defendants and their intentions. They allege also that a bylaw amendment passed by CSX on February 4 concerning shareholder special meetings violates Section 13.1-680 of the Virginia Stock Corporation Act.

Discussion

Section 13(d)

The Williams Act, which enacted what now is Section 13(d) of the Exchange Act, was passed to address the increasing frequency with which hostile takeovers were being used to effect changes in corporate control.[149] Section 13(d)

---

[149] See Act of July 29, 1968, Pub. L. No. 90-439, § 2, 82 Stat. 454 (1968). Senator Williams opened the hearings on the legislation by stating that filling the large gap in the disclosure requirements of the securities laws, a step already taken at that point by several other countries, would ensure that

"[a]ll will be able to deal in the securities markets knowing that all of the pertinent facts are available. This is the premise under which our securities markets are supposed to work. Following this premise they have thrived and prospered over the years. Now is the time to eliminate the last remaining areas where full disclosure is necessary but not yet available."

Full Disclosure of Corporate Equity Ownership and in Corporate Takeover Bids: Hearing in particular was adopted "to alert the marketplace to every large, rapid aggregation or accumulation of securities, regardless of technique employed, which might represent a potential shift in corporate control."[150]

*   *   *

In order to prevent circumvention of Section 13(d)(1), Section 13(d)(3) further provides that "[w]hen two or more persons act as a partnership, limited partnership, syndicate, or other group for the purpose of acquiring, holding, or disposing of securities of an issuer, such syndicate or group shall be deemed a 'person' for the purposes of this subsection."

The heart of the dispute presently before the Court concerns whether (1) TCI's investments in cash-settled TRSs referencing CSX shares conferred beneficial ownership of those shares upon TCI, and (2) TCI and 3G formed a group prior to December 12, 2007.

A.   Beneficial Ownership

The concept of "beneficial ownership" is the foundation of the Williams Act and thus critical to the achievement of its goal of providing transparency to the marketplace.[153] Although Congress did not define the term, its intention manifestly was that the phrase be construed broadly.[154] The SEC did so in Rule 13d-3, which provides in relevant part:

> "(a) For the purposes of sections 13(d) and 13(g) of the Act a beneficial owner of a security includes any person who, directly or indirectly, through any contract, arrangement, understanding, relationship, or otherwise has or shares:
>
> > "(1) Voting power which includes the power to vote, or to direct the voting of, such security; and/or,
> >
> > "(2) Investment power which includes the power to dispose, or to direct the disposition of, such security.

Before the Subcomm. on Securities of the S. Comm. On Banking and Currency, 90th Cong., 1st Sess. 2-3 (1967) (statement of Sen. Williams, Chairman, Senate Subcomm. on Securities).

[150]   *GAF Corp. v. Milstein,* 453 F.2d 709, 717 (2d Cir. 1971), *cert. denied,* 406 U.S. 910, 92 S. Ct. 1610, 31 L. Ed. 2d 821 (1972).

[153]   *See Takeover Bids: Hearing Before the Subcomm. on Commerce and Finance of the H. Comm. on Interstate and Foreign Commerce,* 90th Cong., 2d Sess. 40-41 (1968) (statement of Manuel F. Cohen, Chairman, Securities and Exchange Commission) ("[B]eneficial ownership is the test. [The acquiring entity] might try to get around it, and that would be a violation of law, but the legal requirement is beneficial ownership.").

[154]   *See, e.g., Wellman v. Dickinson,* 682 F.2d 355, 365-66 (2d Cir. 1982) (rejecting narrow construction of § 13(d)(3) in light of legislative history), *cert. denied* 460 U.S. 1069, 103 S. Ct. 1522, 75 L. Ed. 2d 946 (1983).

"(b) Any person who, directly or indirectly, creates or uses a trust, proxy, power of attorney, pooling arrangement or any other contract, arrangement, or device with the purpose of [*sic*] effect of divesting such person of beneficial ownership of a security or preventing the vesting of such beneficial ownership as part of a plan or scheme to evade the reporting requirements of section 13(d) or (g) of the Act shall be deemed for purposes of such sections to be the beneficial owner of such security."

The SEC intended Rule 13d-3(a) to provide a "broad definition" of beneficial ownership so as to ensure disclosure "from all those persons who have the ability to change or influence control." This indeed is apparent from the very words of the Rule. By stating that a beneficial owner "includes" rather than "means" any person who comes within the criteria that follow, it made plain that the language that follows does not exhaust the circumstances in which one might come within the term. The phrases "directly or indirectly" and "any contract, arrangement, understanding, relationship, or otherwise" reinforce that point and demonstrate the focus on substance rather than on form or on the legally enforceable rights of the putative beneficial owner. It therefore" is not surprising that the SEC, at the very adoption of Rule 13d-3, stated that the determination of beneficial ownership under Rule 13d-3(a) requires

"[a]n analysis of all relevant facts and circumstances in a particular situation . . . in order to identify each person possessing the requisite voting power or investment power. For example, for purposes of the rule, the mere possession of the legal right to vote securities under applicable state or other law . . . may not be determinative of who is a beneficial owner of such securities inasmuch as another person or persons may have the power whether legal, economic, or otherwise, to direct such voting.

Nor does Rule 13d-3(a) exhaust the Commission's efforts to cast a very broad net to capture all situations in which the marketplace should be alerted to circumstances that might result in a change in corporate control. Rule 13d-3(b) was adopted so that Rule 13d-3(a) "cannot be circumvented by an arrangement to divest a person of beneficial ownership or to prevent the vesting of beneficial ownership as part of a plan or scheme to evade the reporting requirements of [S]ection 13(d)."

With these considerations in mind, the Court turns to CSX's contentions. It first considers whether TCI had beneficial ownership, within the meaning of Rule 13d-3(a), of the shares of CSX stock referenced by its swap agreements and held by its counterparties by considering the facts and circumstances surrounding those contracts. It then turns to the question of whether TCI, assuming it were not a beneficial owner of the hedge shares under Rule 13d-3(a), nevertheless would be deemed a beneficial owner under Rule 13d-3(b) because it used the TRSs as part of a plan or scheme to evade the disclosure requirements of Section 13(d) by avoiding the vesting of beneficial ownership in TCI.

1. Rule 13d-3(a)

The contracts embodying TCI's swaps did not give TCI any legal rights with respect to the voting or disposition of the CSX shares referenced therein. Nor did they require that its short counterparties acquire CSX shares to hedge their positions. But the beneficial ownership

> "inquiry focuses on any relationship that, as a factual matter, confers on a person a *significant ability to affect* how voting power or investment power will be exercised, because it is primarily designed to ensure timely disclosure of market-sensitive data about changes in the identity of those who are able, as a practicable matter, to influence the use of that power."

It therefore is important to consider whether TCI's TRSs contemplated that its counterparties would hedge their positions with CSX shares and, if so, whether TCI had "a significant ability to affect how voting power or investment power will be exercised."

a.   *Investment Power*

TCI acknowledges, as it must, that its swaps contemplated the possibility that the counterparties might -- indeed would -- hedge by acquiring physical shares. It emphasizes, however, that they were under no contractual obligation to do so and, indeed, had other means of hedging their short positions. Moreover, TCI asserts that it had no influence over how its counterparties disposed of physical shares used to hedge a swap, if any, at the time of termination. TCI therefore maintains that it had no investment power over any shares used to hedge its swaps.

TCI correctly describes the legal instruments constituting the swaps. They do not require the counterparties to hedge their positions by purchasing CSX stock and do not in terms address the question of how the counterparties will dispose of their hedges at the conclusion of the swaps. But the evidence is overwhelming that these counterparties in fact hedged the short positions created by the TRSs with TCI by purchasing shares of CSX common stock. As the charts set forth in Appendix 1 show, they did so on virtually a share-for-share basis and in each case on the day or the day following the commencement of each swap.[161]

This is precisely what TCI contemplated and, indeed, intended. None of these counterparties is in the business, so far as running its swap desk is concerned, of taking on the stupendous risks entailed in holding unhedged short (or long) positions in significant percentages of the shares of listed companies. As a practical

---

[161]   Four of the counterparties -- Citigroup, Deutsche Bank, Morgan Stanley, and UBS -- purchased shares to hedge its corresponding swap short position every time they and TCI entered into a TRS. *See* Subrahmanyam Rebuttal Report, at 12. Deutsche Bank in each case did so on the same day on which the TRS was transacted. *See id.* at 12. Merrill Lynch hedged fifteen of its sixteen swaps by purchasing an equivalent number of matching shares, all on the same day as the swap transaction, and Credit Suisse hedged fourteen of its sixteen swaps in the same manner, all on the same day as the swaps. *Id.* (No data were provided for Goldman or J.P. Morgan.)

matter, the Court finds that their positions could not be hedged through the use of other derivatives. Thus, it was inevitable that they would hedge the TCI swaps by purchasing CSX shares.

TCI knew that the banks would behave in this manner and therefore sought at the outset to spread its TRS agreements across a number of counterparties so as to avoid pushing any counterparty, individually, across the 5 percent threshold that would have triggered an obligation on the counterparty's part to disclose its position under Regulation 13D. This would have been a cause for concern only if TCI understood that its counterparties, although not legally obligated to do so, in fact would hedge by purchasing CSX shares equal or substantially equal to the shares referenced by the TCI swaps.

Moreover, TCI understood that there were advantages to TCI of its short counterparties hedging with physical shares. The fact that these are nominally cash-settled TRSs does not necessarily mean that they all will be settled for cash. TCI and its counterparties have the ability to agree to unwind the swaps in kind, i.e., by delivery of the shares to TCI at the conclusion of each transaction, as indeed commonly occurs. That simple fact means that the hedge positions of the counterparties hang like the sword of Damocles over the neck of CSX. Once the Hart-Scott-Rodino waiting period expired, nothing more was required to move the legal ownership of the hedge shares from the banks to TCI than the stroke of a pen or the transmission of an email. This greatly enhances TCI's leverage over CSX, even if it never settles any of the TRSs for cash, as indeed has been the case to date. And TCI so views the realities as evidenced by Amin's statement to CSX that TCI's swap position could be converted to shares at any time as well as his assertion on February 15, 2007, that TCI "owned" a quantity of shares that clearly included the shares held by its counterparties.

The corollary to the bank's behavior at the front end of these transactions, viz. purchasing physical shares to hedge risk, is that the banks would sell those shares at the conclusion of the swaps (assuming cash settlement) so as to avoid the risk that holding the physical shares would entail once the downside protection of the swap was removed. And that is exactly what happened here. With very minor exceptions, whenever TCI terminated a swap, the counterparty sold the same number of physical shares that were referenced in the unwound swap and it did so on the same day that the swap was terminated. Citigroup, Credit Suisse, Deutsche Bank, Goldman, and Morgan Stanley did precisely this, as did Merrill Lynch and UBS save that (1) Merrill Lynch's sales on a few occasions involved slightly different numbers of shares, and (2) UBS on five occasions sold on the day following the termination of a swap.

To be sure, there is no evidence that TCI explicitly directed the banks to purchase the hedge shares upon entering into the swaps or to sell them upon termination. Nor did it direct the banks to dispose of their hedge shares by any particular means. But that arguably is not dispositive.

On this record, it is quite clear that TCI significantly influenced the banks to purchase the CSX shares that constituted their hedges because the banks, as a practical matter and as TCI both knew and desired, were compelled to do so. It significantly influenced the banks to sell the hedge shares when the swaps were unwound for the same reasons.

b.   Voting Power

There is no evidence that TCI and any of its counterparties had explicit agreements that the banks would vote their hedge shares in a certain way. Moreover, the policies and practices of the counterparties with respect to voting hedge shares vary. But these are not the only pertinent considerations.

(1)   Deutsche Bank

Between October and November 2007, TCI moved swaps referencing 28.4 million and 18.0 million shares into Deutsche Bank and Citigroup, respectively, while leaving swaps referencing 1,000 shares with each of its remaining six counterparties. Hohn offered two reasons for doing so.

First, he said that he felt that commercial banks, which are backed by governmental institutions, entailed less credit risk than investment banks. Second, he conceded that he picked Deutsche Bank and Citigroup --as opposed to other commercial banks -- because he thought that "would be beneficial in terms of a potential vote of any hedge shares in a potential proxy fight." [171]

Hohn's credit risk argument is not entirely persuasive. Assuming *arguendo* that the commercial banks in general were safer than investment banks, it was by no means clear in November 2007 that Citigroup was not a credit risk, notwithstanding its backing by the Federal Reserve. But it is unnecessary to pause on that point, as it is entirely clear that the move into at least Deutsche Bank was made substantially out of Hohn's belief that he could influence the voting of the shares it held to hedge TCI's swaps. As an initial matter, Hohn was well aware that Austin Friars, a hedge fund within Deutsche Bank, held a proprietary position in CSX common stock. From at least March 2007, when Austin Friars invited TCI to submit questions for and listen in on the John Snow call, the two funds shared a common interest in taking a railroad private. Nor was this the first time that they had shared detailed information about positions or plans. Hohn believed that TCI could exploit this relationship to influence how Austin Friars, and in turn how Deutsche Bank, voted its CSX shares. But there is considerably more to the Deutsche Bank situation than Austin Friars.

CSX initially set the record date for voting at its annual meeting as February 27, 2008. Immediately before that record date, Deutsche Bank owned 28.4 million shares to hedge its short position created by its TCI TRSs. Immediately preceding and following the record date, there were large and aberrant movements of CSX shares into and out of Deutsche Bank's hands. CSX argues that these movements show that Deutsche Bank (1) had sought to boost revenues by loaning the shares in its hedge positions, presumably to short sellers, (2) recalled the loans so that it would own the shares on the record date and thus be entitled to vote them, (3) wished to vote those shares pursuant to an arrangement with TCI, and

(4) then reloaned the shares immediately after the record date.

TCI would have the Court reject this scenario as speculative. It argues that the record date for voting coincided closely with the record date determining the right to receive dividends and that it would have been quite natural for Deutsche Bank to have acted to ensure its receipt of those funds. Moreover, it argues that Deutsche Bank witnesses denied that any recall occurred.

TCI's argument falls considerably short. For one thing, CSX adjourned its annual meeting and changed the record date after the record date for payment of a dividend had passed. There is no evidence that the record date for the dividend was changed. Nevertheless, a similar influx and outflow of shares took place around the adjourned record date. In consequence, the desire to receive the dividend is not a likely explanation for what transpired. Moreover, the bank witnesses upon whom TCI relies in fact lacked any personal knowledge of the material facts.

In the last analysis, the question whether there was an agreement -explicit or implicit - between Deutsche Bank and TCI with respect to the voting of the shares is a close one. In view of the grounds on which the Court ultimately disposes of this case, however, it is unnecessary to make a finding on the point.

(2) All of the Counterparties

The Court is not persuaded that there was any agreement or understanding between TCI and any of the other banks with respect to the voting of their hedge shares. But the SEC has made plain that a party has voting power over a share under Rule 13d-3(a)(1) if that party has the "ability to control or *influence* the voting ... of the securities."[182] So the question of influence must be considered with respect to all of the banks.

As an initial matter, TCI, which knew that the banks would hedge the swaps by purchasing physical shares, could and at least to some extent did select counterparties by taking their business to institutions it thought would be most likely to vote with TCI in a proxy contest. D.F. King's "Preliminary Vote Outlook" presentation concerning the proxy contest indicates that certain types of investors adhere to particular voting patterns in contested elections and are influenced by the recommendations made by institutional proxy advisory firms such as RiskMetrics (formerly ISS). Although D.F. King was clear that it could not guarantee the manner in which a particular investor would vote, patterns of behavior made it possible for TCI to predict the likelihood of that vote and place its swap transactions accordingly.

Further, some of the banks' policies gave TCI the power to prevent a share from being voted. Credit Suisse, for example, appears to follow a policy of not

---

[182]   Interpretive Release on Rules Applicable to Insider Reporting and Trading, Exchange Act Release No. 34-18114, 46 Fed. Reg. 48,147 (Oct. 1, 1981) (emphasis added). *See also Wellman*, 682 F.2d at 365 n.12 (beneficial ownership not defined by Rule 13d-3 "solely as present voting power").

voting its hedge shares if it is solicited by its counterparty in a contested situation. In such instances, then, TCI could ensure that that bank's hedge shares would not be voted against it by the simple expedient of soliciting its counterparty. Thus, by entering into a TRS with Credit Suisse, TCI was in a position to ensure that Credit Suisse would purchase shares that otherwise might have been voted against TCI in a proxy fight and then to ensure that those shares would not be so voted. While this would not be as favorable a result as dictating a vote in its favor, it would be better than leaving the votes of those shares to chance.

Finally, the fact that TCI thought it could influence Citigroup at least suggests that its relationship with Citigroup permitted it to do so. Nevertheless, the proof on this point is not sufficient to find that TCI in fact had that ability.

    c.   *Synthesis*

In the last analysis, there are substantial reasons for concluding that TCI is the beneficial owner of the CSX shares held as hedges by its short counterparties. The definition of "beneficial ownership" in Rule 13d-3(a) is very broad, as is appropriate to its object of ensuring disclosure "from all . . . persons who have the ability [even] to . . . influence control." It does not confine itself to "the mere possession of the legal right to vote or direct the acquisition or disposition of] securities," but looks instead to all of the facts and circumstances to identify situations in which one has even the ability to influence voting, purchase, or sale decisions of its counterparties by "legal, economic, or other[]" means.

On this record, TCI manifestly had the economic ability to cause its short counterparties to buy and sell the CSX shares. The very nature of the TRS transactions, as a practical matter, required the counterparties to hedge their short exposures. And while there theoretically are means of hedging that do not require the purchase of physical shares, in the situation before the Court it is perfectly clear that the purchase of physical shares was the only practical alternative. Indeed, TCI effectively has admitted as much. It did so by spreading its swap transactions among eight counterparties to avoid any one hitting the 5 percent disclosure threshold and thus triggering its own reporting obligation - a concern that was relevant only because TCI knew that the counterparties were hedging by buying shares. And it did so in closing argument, where its counsel said that the banks' purchases of CSX shares were "the natural consequence" of the swap transactions. [188] Thus, TCI patently had the power to cause the counterparties to buy CSX. At the very least, it had the power to influence them to do so. And once the counterparties bought the shares, TCI had the practical ability to cause them to sell simply by unwinding the swap transactions. Certainly the banks had no intention of allowing their swap desks to hold the unhedged long positions that would have resulted from the unwinding of the swaps.

The voting situation is a bit murkier, but there nevertheless is reason to believe that TCI was in a position to influence the counterparties, especially Deutsche Bank, with respect to the exercise of their voting rights.

TCI nevertheless argues strenuously against a finding that it has beneficial ownership of the shares, focusing heavily on the fact that it had no legal right to direct its short counterparties to buy or sell shares or to vote them in any particular way, indeed at all.[189] Some *amici*, more cautiously, urge that any finding of beneficial ownership be rooted in unique facts of this case to avoid upsetting what they say is the settled expectation of the marketplace that equity swaps, *in and of themselves*, do not confer beneficial ownership of the referenced shares. They contend that a broader ruling could have extensive implications and that the subject therefore is dealt with more appropriately by administrative agency rule making than case-by-case adjudication. And the SEC Division of Corporation Finance argues - perhaps inconsistently with some of the Commission's past statements about the breadth of the definition of beneficial ownership - that there is no beneficial ownership where the short counterparties buy, sell, or vote their hedge shares as a result of their own economic incentives and not pursuant to legal obligations owed to their long counterparties, although it does not comment on the facts of this case. The Division, moreover, suggests that a contrary ruling would be novel and upset settled expectations of the market.

The focus on TCI's legal rights under its swap contracts, while those rights certainly are relevant, exalts form over substance. The securities markets operate in the real world, not in a law school contracts classroom. Any determination of beneficial ownership that failed to take account of the practical realities of that world would be open to the gravest abuse. Indeed, this Court is not alone in recognizing that abuses would be facilitated by a regime that did not require disclosure of the sort that would be required if "beneficial ownership" were construed as advocated by CSX.[191]

---

[189]   Defendants rely on an SEC interpretive release in which the Commission took the position that "[a] purchaser of a cash-settled security future (*i.e.*, a security future that, by its terms, must be settled by a cash payment) would not count the equity securities underlying the contract for purposes of determining whether he or she is subject to the Regulation 13D reporting requirements, because he or she does not have the right to acquire beneficial ownership of the underlying security." Commission Guidance on the Application of Certain Provisions to Trading in Security Futures Products, 67 Fed. Reg. 43,234, 43,240 (June 27, 2002) (listed as an interpretive release at 17 C.F.R. pts. 231 and 241).

As an initial matter, no one suggests that this interpretation resolves the question before this Court. The interpretive release involved only cash-settled securities futures, which are impersonal exchange traded transactions, and at least to that extent, unlike cash-settled equity swaps. Moreover, there is no evidence that the Commission intended this guidance to apply outside the context of cash-settled securities futures. In any case, in view of the fact that the matter is being decided on other grounds, this interpretation need not be addressed at greater length.

[191]   *See, e.g.*, Henry Hu & Bernard Black, *Equity and Debt Decoupling and Empty Voting II: Importance and Extensions*, 156 U. PENN. L. REV. 625, 735-37 (2008) (assuming that equity swaps do not give the long party beneficial ownership, they can be used to secure effective control without disclosure otherwise required by § 13(d)). Similarly,

Moreover, the Court is inclined to the view that the Cassandra-like predictions of dire consequences of holding that TCI has beneficial ownership under Rule 13d-3(a) have been exaggerated. For one thing, there is no reason to believe that there are many situations in which the 5 percent reporting threshold under Section 13(d) would be triggered by such a ruling. The overwhelming majority of swap transactions would proceed as before without any additional Regulation 13D or G reporting requirements. The issue here, moreover, is novel and hardly settled. And markets can well adapt regardless of how it ultimately is resolved. Indeed, the United Kingdom reportedly now requires disclosure of economic stakes greater than 1 percent in companies involved in takeovers and is considering requiring disclosure at the 3 percent level in other companies, levels lower than would be required to trigger Section 13(d), assuming that the TRSs here fall within Rule 13d-3(a). Yet there is no reason to believe that the sky has fallen, or is likely to fall, in London.

Nor do potentially broad implications or any supposed advantage of administrative rule making over adjudication permit a court to decline to decide an issue that must be decided in order to resolve a case before it. But it is equally true that courts should decide no more than is essential to resolve their cases.

In this case, it is not essential to decide the beneficial ownership question under Rule 13d-3(a). As is discussed immediately below, TCI used the TRSs with the purpose and effect of preventing the vesting of beneficial ownership of the referenced shares in TCI as part of a plan or scheme to evade the reporting requirements of Section 13(d). Under Rule 13d-3(b), TCI, if it is not a beneficial owner under rule 13d-3(a), therefore is deemed - on the facts of this case - to beneficially own those shares. The Court therefore does not rule on the legal question whether TCI is a beneficial owner under Section 13d-3(a).

2.   *Rule 13d-3(b)*

In construing any statute or rule, the Court is governed by well-established principles. It first must examine "the language of the provision at issue," which governs "'unless that meaning would lead to absurd results.'" In addition, the provision "should be construed so that effect is given to all its provisions, so that no part will be inoperative or superfluous, void or insignificant, and so that one section will not destroy another unless the provision is the result of obvious mistake or error."

We begin with the language. Rule 13d-3(b) provides:

"Any person who, directly or indirectly, [1] creates or uses a trust, proxy, power of attorney, pooling arrangement or any other contract, arrangement,

---

professor and former SEC commissioner Joseph Grundfest and other academics have written that "[i]n the context of this case, the . . . integrity of the stock market was undermined and an uneven playing field was created." *See* Letter from Joseph Grundfest, Henry Hu, and Marti Subrahmanyam to Brian Cartwright, General Counsel of the SEC (June 2, 2008), at 13.

or device [2] with the purpose of [*sic*] effect of divesting such person of beneficial ownership of a security or preventing the vesting of such beneficial ownership [3] as part of a plan or scheme to evade the reporting requirements of section 13(d) or (g) of the Act shall be deemed for purposes of such sections to be the beneficial owner of such security."

Thus, the Rule by its plain terms is triggered when three elements are satisfied:

- the use of a contract, arrangement, or device

- with the purpose or effect of divesting such person of beneficial ownership of a security or preventing the vesting of such beneficial ownership

- as part of a plan or scheme to evade the reporting requirements of Section 13(d) or (g).

It is undisputed that TCI's cash-settled TRSs are contracts. The first element therefore concededly is satisfied.

The evidence that TCI created and used the TRSs, at least in major part, for the purpose of preventing the vesting of beneficial ownership of CSX shares in TCI and as part of a plan or scheme to evade the reporting requirements of Section 13(d) is overwhelming.   Joe O'Flynn, the chief financial officer of TCI Fund told its board, albeit not in the specific context of CSX, that one of the reasons for using swaps is "the ability to purchase without disclosure to the market or the company." TCI emails discussed the need to make certain that its counterparties stayed below 5 percent physical share ownership, this in order to avoiding triggering a disclosure obligation on the part of a counterparty. TCI admitted that one of its motivations in avoiding disclosure was to avoid paying a higher price for the shares of CSX, which would have been the product of front-running that it expected would occur if its interest in CSX were disclosed to the market generally. NCI Indeed, TCI acquired only approximately 4.5 percent in physical CSX shares to remain safely below the 5 percent reporting requirement until it was ready to disclose its position.

To be sure, there is evidence that TCI argues points in the opposite direction. It did disclose to CSX the fact that it had exposure to its stock well before it made a Schedule 13D filing. But that does not carry the day. Telling an issuer that an investor has exposure to its stock is quite a different matter than timely disclosing to the marketplace generally the details of the investor's position, its plans and intentions, its contracts and arrangements with respect to the issuer's securities, and its financing and then keeping that information up to date as Regulation 13D requires. For one thing, the market in general does not necessarily know even what the issuer knows. And the issuer is left to guess as to many of the important matters that compliance with Regulation 13D requires. Here, TCI's limited disclosure to CSX and its concealment of broader, more timely, and more accurate information from the marketplace served its objectives. It exerted pressure on CSX, a pressure that was enhanced by the lack of complete information. And it kept the marketplace entirely and, after CSX filed its Form 10-Q, largely in the dark, thus serving TCI's interest in permitting it to build its position without running up the price of the stock. In all the circumstances, the Court finds that each of the elements of Rule 13d-3(b) is satisfied here.

This outcome is supported by the views of the SEC's Division of Corporation Finance as the Court understands them. While the Division did not comment upon or attempt to analyze the facts of this case in light of governing legal standards, its *amicus* letter appears to take two positions. First, it states the view that "the long party's underlying motive for entering into the swap transaction generally is not a basis for determining whether there is 'a plan or scheme to evade.'" It goes on to say that it believes "that the mental state contemplated by the words 'plan or scheme to evade' is generally the intent to enter into an arrangement that creates a false appearance." It states that "a person who entered into a swap would be a beneficial owner under Rule 13d-3(b) if it were determined that the person did so with the intent to create the false appearance of non-ownership of a security." But it adds that it "cannot rule out the possibility that, in some unusual circumstances, a plan or scheme to evade the beneficial ownership provisions of Rule 13d-3 might exist where the evidence does not indicate a false appearance or sham transaction." Having said that, however, the letter concludes that "as a general matter, a person that does nothing more than enter into an equity swap should not be found to have engaged in an evasion of the reporting requirements."

As an initial matter, no one suggests that TCI did "nothing more than enter into an equity swap." At a minimum, it entered into the TRSs rather than buying stock for the purpose, perhaps among others, of avoiding the disclosure requirements of Section 13(d) by preventing the 68 vesting of beneficial ownership in TCI.

Passing on to its other point, the Division's assertion that "a person who entered into a swap would be a beneficial owner under Rule 13d-3(b) if it were determined that the person did so with the intent to create the false appearance of non-ownership of a security" suffers from some degree of ambiguity. On the one hand, the statement may be intended merely to illustrate a specific intent that would satisfy the test, without intending to exhaust the possibilities. On the other, it may intend to convey the thought that an intent to create a false appearance of non-ownership is indispensable to a Rule 13d-3(b) finding. Two considerations persuade the Court that the former is the case.

First, the Division declined to "rule out the possibility that . . . a plan or scheme to evade . . . might exist [without] a false appearance or sham transaction." It follows that it cannot be saying that, in its view, a false appearance of non-ownership is a necessary condition for application of Rule 13d-3(b).

Second, reading Rule 13d-3(b) as requiring an intent to create a false appearance of non-ownership would violate a fundamental principle of statutory construction. An appearance of non-ownership cannot be false unless one in fact is at least a beneficial owner. That beneficial ownership would satisfy Rule 13d-3(a), thus making Rule 13d-3(b) superfluous. In consequence, Rule 13d-3 as a whole is inconsistent with any view that a false appearance of non-ownership is a prerequisite to application of Rule 13d-3(b).

This leaves us with the Division's more likely position, viz. that Rule 13d-3(b) is satisfied only where the actor intends to create some false appearance, albeit not necessarily a false appearance of non-ownership. But false appearance of what?

The goal of Section 13(d) "is to alert the marketplace to every large, rapid aggregation or accumulation of securities . . . which might represent a potential shift in corporate control." In consequence, the natural reading is that the Division refers to a false appearance that no such accumulation is taking place. Put another way, Rule 13d-3(b) applies where one enters into a transaction with the intent to create the false appearance that there is no large accumulation of securities that might have a potential for shifting corporate control by evading the disclosure requirements of Section 13(d) or (g) through preventing the vesting of beneficial ownership in the actor.

If that is what the Division means, then its proposed standard is more than satisfied in this case. TCI intentionally entered into the TRSs, with the purpose and intent of preventing the vesting of beneficial ownership in TCI, as part of a plan or scheme to evade the reporting requirements of Section 13(d) and thus concealed precisely what Section 13(d) was intended to force into the open. And if this is not what the Division means, the Division's argument would be unpersuasive. After all, there is not one word in Section 13(d) or in Rule 13d-3 that supports a requirement of an intent to create a false appearance of non-ownership if that term requires anything more than concealment of the sort of secret market accumulations that went on here.

Undaunted, TCI argues that it did not trigger Rule 13d-3(b). It relies in part on a letter from Professor Bernard Black to the SEC in which the professor argued that "it must be permissible for an investor to acquire equity swaps, rather than shares, in part -- or indeed entirely -- *because* share ownership is disclosable under § 13(d) while equity swaps are not." He bases this argument on the premise that "the underlying [i.e., evasive] activity must involve holding a position which is 'beneficial ownership' under the *statute* (Exchange Act § 13(d) or (g)), but would otherwise fall outside the *rule* -- outside the SEC's effort to define the concept of beneficial ownership elsewhere in Rule 13d-3." With respect, the Court finds the argument unpersuasive.

As an initial matter, the SEC, in the Court's view, has the power to treat as beneficial ownership a situation that would not fall within the statutory meaning of that term. Section 23(a) of the Exchange Act grants the Commission the "power to make such rules and regulations as may be necessary or appropriate to implement the provisions of this chapter for which [it is] responsible ..." The validity of a rule or regulation promulgated under such a grant of authority will be sustained so long as it is "reasonably related to the purposes of the enabling legislation."

The purpose of Section 13(d) is to alert shareholders of "every large, rapid aggregation or accumulation of securities, regardless of technique employed, which might represent a potential shift in corporate control." Rule 13d-3(b) was promulgated to further this purpose by preventing circumvention of Rule 13d-3 with arrangements designed to avoid disclosure obligations by preventing the vesting of beneficial ownership as defined elsewhere - in other words, where there is accumulation of securities by any means with a potential shift of corporate control, but no beneficial ownership. As Rule 13d-3(b) therefore is reasonably related to the purpose of the statute, it is a perfectly appropriate exercise of the Commission's authority even where it reaches arrangements that otherwise would not amount to beneficial ownership.

Second, while it may be debated whether the term "beneficial ownership" as used in the Williams Act is broader than or coextensive with the same language as used in Rule 13d-3(a),[213] one thing is quite clear. If Rule 13d-3(b) reaches only situations that involve beneficial ownership, then it reaches only situations that are reached by Rule 13d-3(a). Professor Black's view thus would render Rule 13d-3(b) superfluous.

* * *

In sum, the Court finds that TCI created and used the TRSs with the purpose and effect of preventing the vesting of beneficial ownership in TCI as part of a plan or scheme to evade the reporting requirements of Section 13(d). Under the plain language of Rule 13d-3(b), it thus is deemed to be a beneficial owner of the shares held by its counterparties to hedge their short exposures created by the TRSs.

[The court determined that TCI and 3G formed a group as part of their plan or scheme to evade the reporting requirements of section 13(d), and that they did not disclose their joint ownership within ten days as required by the Act. The court denied CSX's request for an injunction that would prohibit the voting of any of the shares owned by the defendants at the 2008 annual meeting on the basis that CSX failed to show irreparable harm.]

Add at the end of Note beginning on page 1010:

Skeen was reinforced in McMullin v. Beran, 765 A.2d 910, 926 (Del. 2000), where the court stated: "In Skeen, it was argued that the minority

---

[213]   The language of the Rule defines the term "[f]or the purposes of sections 13(d) and 13(g) of the Act." 17 C.F.R. § 240.13d-3(a). While the use in the Rule of the term "includes," *inter alia*, makes clear that Rule 13d-3(a)(1) and (2) are not the only criteria that define "beneficial ownership," Rule 13d-3(a) as a whole appears quite plainly to reflect the Commission's intent to define the term exhaustively for purposes of the statute. Curiously, however, the Division's *amicus* letter, without citation of authority, states that the Division "believes that Rule 13d-3, properly construed, is narrower in coverage than the statute."

shareholders should have been given all of the financial data they would need if they were making an independent determination of fair value. We decline to establish 'a new disclosure standard where appraisal is an option.' [citations omitted]".

Some decisions of the Chancery Court have observed this rule. In In Re Siliconix Inc. Shareholder Litigation, 2001 Del. Ch. LEXIS 83, Vice Chancellor Noble, dismissed a complaint that the Schedule 14D-9 prepared by the subsidiary in response to a parent's tender offer did not disclose "details and assumptions" relating to projections. In rejecting this claim, the court noted that there was no substantial likelihood shown by plaintiffs that the details and assumptions would "significantly alter the total mix already provided" to shareholders. The court concluded that the plaintiff failed to show that these details and assumptions "justify overcoming the reluctance of courts to order disclosure of 'soft information.' Such information might be 'helpful,' but here it has not been shown to be material." *Id.* at *41-42.

A significant departure appears in the opinion of Vice Chancellor Strine in In Re Netsmart Technologies, Inc. Shareholders Litigation, 924 A.2d 171 (Del. Ch. 2007). Vice Chancellor Strine's jurisprudence should be put in the context of his rejection of the Supreme Court's materiality standard in Skeen in his opinion in In Re Pure Resources, Inc., Shareholders Litigation, 808 A.2d 421 (Del. Ch. 2002). Pure involved a transaction with a controlling shareholder that exercised its control. Unocal Corp. owned 65% of Pure's stock and controlled its board. When Unocal determined to acquire all minority shares, it simply announced the terms of an exchange offer, and never varied them. When Pure's board selected a special committee to evaluate the fairness of the terms, the board determined to limit the power of the special committee, so that it could not seek alternative transactions or resist the offer by adopting takeover defenses. 808 A.2d at 430-31. The court concluded that the special committee was unwilling to challenge Unocal as aggressively as it would have challenged a third-party bidder, *id.* at 431, but the special committee nevertheless recommended that shareholders reject the offer. *Id.* at 432. The Schedule 14D-9 did "not disclose any substantive portions of the work" of the investment bankers who served as advisors. Vice Chancellor Strine also stressed that in transactions with controlling shareholders, "they have large informational advantages that can only be imperfectly overcome by the special committee process, which almost invariably involves directors who are not involved in the day-to-day management of the subsidiary", so that the work of investment bankers becomes even more important, as does the need to disclose it in full detail. *Id.* at 450.

Vice Chancellor Strine's opinion disagrees with opinions of the Delaware Supreme Court, as he candidly concedes. *Id.* at 78-79. "Fearing stepping on the SEC's toes and worried about encouraging prolix disclosures, the Delaware courts have been reluctant to require informative, succinct disclosure of investment banker analyses in circumstances in which the bankers' views about value have been cited as justifying the recommendation of the board." *Id.* at 79-80. Vice Chancellor

Strine claims an ambivalence in recent Delaware Supreme Court opinions which is less than obvious upon closer inspection. In Skeen v. Jo-Ann Stores, Inc., *supra*, plaintiff's complaints were similar to those involved here – the absence of a summary of methodologies used, ranges of values generated by the bankers and the absence of management's projections of future performance, *inter alia*. The Supreme Court rejected these claims on materiality grounds, stating that:

> "it ignores settled law. Omitted facts are not material simply because they might be helpful. To be actionable, there must be a substantial likelihood that the undisclosed information would significantly alter the total mix of information already provided. The complaint alleges no facts suggesting that the undisclosed information is inconsistent with, or otherwise significantly differs from, the disclosed information. Appellants merely allege that the added information would be helpful in valuing the company." 750 A.2d at 1174.

Perhaps because Skeen did not support Vice Chancellor Strine's conclusions in Pure, he claimed that McMullin v. Beran, 765 A.2d 910 (Del. 2000), offers a "conflicting" impulse on additional disclosure of investment banker analyses. McMullin involved a total abdication by a subsidiary's board in the face of its parent's efforts to sell the subsidiary. The subsidiary's board failed to determine whether the offer was fair. Neither the board members nor its nominal financial adviser possessed sufficient information to judge the fairness of the transaction, or to advise shareholders. Not surprisingly, under these circumstances the court refused to dismiss the complaint. As if to reaffirm Skeen and distinguish McMullan, the court stated "In Skeen, it was argued that the minority shareholders should have been given all of the financial data they would need if they were making an independent determination of fair value. We declined to establish 'a new disclosure standard where appraisal is an option.' *We adhere to our holding in Skeen.*" 765 A.2d at 925.

Like McMullin, Netsmart offers a conflict of interest situation, where a management team chose to sell to private equity investors in order to obtain a larger share of the enterprise. Vice Chancellor Strine did not cite the governing law of the Skeen opinion concerning additional disclosures, choosing instead to cite his own opinion in Pure Resources that was critical of the Skeen rule. Noting the informational advantage of management in a leveraged management buyout, he stated that "[i]t would therefore seem to be a genuinely foolish (and arguably unprincipled and unfair) inconsistency to hold that the best estimate of the company's future returns, as generated by management and the Special Committee's investment bank, need not be disclosed when stockholders are being advised to cash out. * * * The conclusion that this omission is material should not be surprising. Once a board breaches a topic in its disclosures, a duty attaches to provide information that is 'materially complete and unbiased by the omission of material facts." 924 A.2d at 203.

Other Chancery Court decisions have continued to follow Skeen. See, e.g., In re Check Free Corp. Shareholders' Litigation, 2007 Del. Ch. LEXIS 148 and

Globis Partners, L.P. v. Plumtree Software, Inc., 2007 Del. Ch. LEXIS 169.